THE STRANGENESS OF THE ORDINARY

THE STRANGENESS OF THE ORDINARY

Problems and Issues in Contemporary Metaphysics

Robert C. Coburn

Rowman & Littlefield Publishers, Inc.

ROWMAN & LITTLEFIELD PUBLISHERS, INC.

Published in the United States of America
by Rowman & Littlefield Publishers, Inc.
8705 Bollman Place, Savage, Maryland 20763

British Cataloging in Publication Information Available

Library of Congress Cataloging-in-Publication Data

Coburn, Robert C.
The strangeness of the ordinary : problems and
issues in contemporary metaphysics / Robert C. Coburn.
p.   cm.
Includes bibliographical references.
1. Metaphysics.   I. Title.
BD111.C584   1990   110—dc20   89–28058 CIP

ISBN 0–8476–7606–7

5   4   3   2   1

Printed in the United States of America

TM The paper used in this publication meets the minimum requirements of
American National Standard for Information Sciences—Permanence of
Paper for Printed Library Materials, ANSI Z39.48–1984.

For Martha

Contents

Reason here seems to be thrown into a kind of amazement and suspense which . . . gives her a diffidence of herself and of the ground on which she treads. She sees a full light which illuminates certain places, but that light borders upon the most profound darkness.
> —David Hume
> *An Inquiry Concerning Human Understanding*

The achievement of [Wittgenstein's] new philosophy is its demonstration of the strangeness of the ordinary.
> —David Pears
> *The False Prison*

Preface

In *Science and the Modern World,* Alfred North Whitehead wrote that mathematics, like Ophelia, is "very charming," "a little mad," but "quite essential to the play."* Metaphysics might well be characterized in similar terms. Its charms are also great. It too is a little mad—some would add "at best." And one can hardly scratch the surface of Western intellectual history without coming upon it in one form or another.

Mathematics and metaphysics share some additional features. One of the more obvious is that the kinds of investigations they involve are carried on without recourse to the careful observation and frequently ingenious experimental work that lies at the heart of empirical sciences like physics and biology. Another is that most people—even many very well educated people—lack even the haziest idea about the sort of work that goes on at the frontiers of mathematics and metaphysics.

In the case of metaphysics, these latter features are probably connected. Metaphysicians, after all, purport to say something about the character of the world in which we live; but since that's what the empirical sciences do, what could the metaphysician possibly be up to? And there is another important source of perplexity about the metaphysical enterprise. The word 'metaphysics' is often used to denote a variety of activities and doctrines that professional philosophers—in general, those with doctorates in philosophy from the major research universities and teaching positions in departments of philosophy in reputable institutions of higher learning—regard as no more

---

*Alfred North Whitehead, *Science and the Modern World* (New York: Mentor Books, 1948), p. 26.

worthy of serious attention than the pseudo-scientific idiocies that fill the pages of the tabloids. Thus, it is easy for nonprofessionals to suppose that serious philosophers at the major universities are engaged in a legitimate enterprise that is continuous with the rubbish that is called 'metaphysics' in the popular press, and it is difficult to see what such an enterprise could possibly be. (People might have a similar problem regarding mathematics if the term 'mathematics' were also used to designate, say, the symbolic gibberish produced by persons suffering a certain form of brain damage.)

Unfortunately, it is not easy to give a brief, yet illuminating, characterization of metaphysics. (The same is true of every serious and highly reticulate intellectual discipline.) The best such account, in my judgment, runs thus. Metaphysics is the discipline that is concerned with a variety of questions and problems that arise when one reflects upon certain notions that pervade everyday thought and discourse— notions such as *time, space, object, property, necessity, possibility, existence, fact, God, consciousness, causality, event, truth, proposition,* and *value.*

This account is relatively unilluminating, of course, because it leaves unclear the questions and problems that metaphysics is concerned with, how reflection upon various of the notions indicated generates the questions and problems, and what procedures the metaphysician follows in trying to answer them.

So far as I can see, there is no way to remedy this defect short of a book. My hope is that the present book will serve this purpose. But I want not only to fill the gaps in the above account of what metaphysics is; I want also to provide a view of this area of philosophy that is wide-ranging without being superficial. I hope too that the reader will come to see how natural and easy it is—indeed how unavoidable it is!—to enter the paths of metaphysical reflection; how captivating are the issues that engage the metaphysician; and, perhaps most important, how close to home the mystery of existence appears once one begins to raise certain obvious questions in connection with remarks (and thoughts) we make (and have) every day of our lives.

I have written mainly for advanced undergraduate and graduate students of philosophy, as well as for professionals both within and outside the discipline of philosophy narrowly understood. In the interest of making the book as widely accessible as possible, I have added a glossary of technical terms. With its help, the book will, I hope, be intelligible to those who have a minimal acquaintance with elementary logic and have had one or two introductory-level philosophy courses based, at least in part, on contemporary sources. A brief list of suggested readings will guide the interested reader to some of the valuable, mainly current, literature on the issues the book treats.

Metaphysical issues arise in virtually every area of philosophy, and since philosophical questions lurk beneath the surface of every intellectual discipline, as well as all the practices and institutions that shape our lives, the problems of metaphysics are vast in number as well as multifarious and ubiquitous. As a consequence, even a book on metaphysics that purports to provide a reasonable overview of the field will necessarily be highly selective in the issues it treats. The topics I have chosen for consideration have been selected for three reasons: (a) all, in one way or another, have deep roots in the metaphysical tradition, (b) all are at the center of some of the best current work in the field, and (c) all are topics that I have found extraordinarily and endlessly fascinating. I hope I have managed to convey why these topics have traditionally been, and continue to be, so enthralling.

Acknowledgments

I have benefited greatly from discussion of many parts of a penulti-mate draft with my friend and former student Clark Shores. Comments on early versions of Chapters 5, 7, and 8 by Marc Cohen, Christine Keyt, and John Boler, respectively, have enabled me to improve these chapters. A version of Chapter 4 was read at North Carolina State University, a version of Chapter 1 at Duke University and Emory University, and a version of part of Chapter 8 at the University of Bergin in Norway. I am grateful for the comments I received from the audiences at these talks. I also received help and stimulation on various of the issues considered in Chapters 1, 4, 5, and 6 from the members of my National Endowment for the Humanities Seminar on "The Metaphysics of Identity" in the summer of 1983.

I am indebted as well to the University of Washington for a sabbatical leave in the 1982–1983 academic year and for a release-time award in the spring of 1985. Without the relatively free stretches of time these leaves made possible, the book would have been written only in certain nonactual possible worlds.

I wish to thank the following publishers and journals for their permission to reprint papers that appear (in slightly altered versions) as Chapters 1, 5, and 7: (1) *Canadian Journal of Philosophy* for the use of "Personal Identity Revisited," 16 (September, 1985); (2) The University of Minnesota Press for the use of "Individual Essences and Possible Worlds," *Midwest Studies in Philosophy,* 11 (1986); and (3) Basil Blackwell Ltd. and *Philosophical Investigations* for the use of "Metaphysical Theology and the Life of Faith," 11 (July, 1988).

Finally, I am grateful to my wife who, with unremitting cheerfulness, spent more hours at the computer deciphering marginally legible scribblings than I wish to contemplate.

CHAPTER ONE

The Persistence of Persons

We frequently make judgments that assert or imply that some person who exists now is the very same person as an individual who existed at some earlier time; that someone has persisted through time, remaining the same individual despite having undergone various changes, sometimes even very dramatic ones, in the intervening period. Thus, we say such things as "The person you see over there leaning against the door is the very one you saw on the tennis courts yesterday," "The first marriage of the woman who was married yesterday lasted 27 years," and "I was a vacuum cleaner salesman in 1951." Such judgments are among the most puzzling we make. They are, to be sure, as common as air, and on the surface are both straightforward and pellucid; yet as soon as we try to understand the nature of the relation that we believe to hold when we "identify" a person who exists now with some person who existed at some earlier time, we fall into deep perplexity. Why this is so I shall try to make clear in the present chapter.

I

When we are first confronted with the question as to the nature of this relation—hereafter R—the following theses might well appear upon reflection to be obvious. First, it might seem that R has to be a "one-one" relation, that is, a relation that can be borne by something to no more than one thing and that no more than one thing can bear to anything. After all, if someone convinces us, for example, that the person over there with the Yo Yo is the person we tripped over yesterday, and that the latter is the realtor we spoke with last year, then we will certainly infer that the person over there with the Yo Yo is the realtor we spoke with last year. Nor will we be in any doubt that the legitimacy of such an inference is explained by the transitivity of the relation in question. Parallel considerations about obviously legitimate inferential patterns suggest that the relation is also symmetrical. Thus, if you convince me that the person before me is the barber who scalped me last week, I shall *eo ipso* be convinced that the barber who scalped me last week is identical with the person before me. And since no one doubts that *NN* is the same person as *NN,* whoever *NN* may be, although it would ordinarily be quite odd to remark upon it, the relation appears to be reflexive as well. A relation that has these features is by definition an equivalence relation. But if the relation in question is an equivalence relation, then it is also a one-one relation. For suppose it were, say, a one-many relation. Then some person who existed at t_i ("*a*" say) could bear it to some person who existed at some later time t_j ("*b*" say), and also to some person who existed at some still later time t_k ("*c*" say), where *b* and *c* are distinct persons. But given that R is an equivalence relation, if *aRb* and *aRc,* then *cRa* and *aRb,* from which it follows that *cRb,* which contradicts the supposition. Similar arguments can be constructed in an obvious way to rule out R's being many-one and many-many.

Second, it might appear obvious that R, like the relations *being the square root of* and *being the (biological) father of,* is an "all-or-nothing" relation in the sense that it does not admit of degrees. This might strike one as obvious because of the doubtful sense of saying things like "He is the same person as the barber you thought you'd murdered last week, although he is less identical with that person than you are with the man he performed his tonsorial outrages upon" and "She is to some degree the same person you played post office with in junior high school, and when I say this I do not mean that she is merely similar in certain respects to the person in question."

Third, one might be strongly inclined to believe that R does not allow of borderline cases and so is neither "vague" nor "open-textured," on the following grounds. It is surely obvious if anything is, one might reflect, that for any person you wish to consider who will exist next week, either that person will be you or it will not be you, and this no matter what circumstances are imagined to surround either you or the person under consideration. What would it be, after all, for some person who will exist next week to satisfy neither description? It seems on the face of it quite inconceivable that she should neither be you nor someone distinct from you. In other words, one might be moved to accept this thesis by the seeming self-evidence of the thought that there are, and can be, no cases concerning which there just is no fact of the matter whether or not a is the same person as b, where a is a person who exists at t_i and b is a person who exists at some later time t_j. It should be noted that one who has such intuitions need not deny that there may well be "decision questions" in this area, that is, questions that can be answered only by making a (more-or-less arbitrary) decision. For the thesis that R is neither vague nor open-textured does not imply that we are always in a position to settle questions concerning the identity through time of persons (hereafter "personal identity" questions). Hence, this thesis is quite compatible with the view that there are conceivable situations in which we could not find out what the relevant facts are and so might, for practical reasons, just have to decide.

Finally, one might feel it is evident (a) that no analysis of R that appeals to empirically discernible connection(s) of the kind we ordinarily take as evidence for personal identity judgments could possibly be adequate, and indeed (b) that no analysis of any kind will do, except a trivial one that presupposes a prior understanding of R. Thus (a) might appear evident because of a sense that any such empirical connection might fail to obtain between a and b, even though b was nonetheless the same person as a. For example, a sufficiently powerful God, one might reflect, could engineer a general resurrection and a Last Judgment of the sinners who had lived and died eons before, despite the fact that these post-resurrection people had newly created bodies, possibly very different psychological features from those they possessed earlier, and no causal connections with their earlier selves. One might also, or alternatively, be moved to accept (a) by the thought that if (a) were false, then R could hardly fail to allow of borderline cases, since notions like spatiotemporal continuity, psychological similarity, and the like, which play a central role in the judgments we appeal to in evidence of personal identity, are vague. But that R should be vague flies in the face of intuitions of the kind mentioned in the preceding paragraph.

The thesis that no analysis of R of any sort will do, except one that is clearly both trivial and circular—(b)—might seem clearly true because the only viable candidate for such an analysis is one that might be stated in either of the following ways: (i) necessarily (a R b iff whatever is true of a at any time is true of b at that time, and conversely); or (ii) necessarily [a R b iff a exists at all and only the times when b exists and (t) (F) (a has property F at t only if b has F at *t,* and conversely)]. This analysis is circular because the conditions in the analysantia obviously involve the idea of a person's existing at different times, and hence the notion of personal identity-through-time. The reason for describing it as trivial is that all it does is to make explicit the bearing of the standard understanding of strict identity that appeals to Leibniz's Law and its converse in the cross-temporal case. Thus, if a and b both exist at t_i, a clearly will be identical with b iff a and b share all their properties in common. But if a exists at t_i and b is a at a later stage of a's history (say at t_j), b must exist at t_i, at every other time at which a exists, and at only the times at which a exists, and b must have every property a has at any time t at that very time.

Let us call the view of one who accepts the foregoing theses "the natural view." Despite its attractiveness, this view is open to an obvious and serious objection. Put in the form of an argument, this objection goes as follows. We frequently have good evidence for the truth of our personal identity judgments, evidence in fact that suffices to justify claims to know that these judgments are correct. But if the natural view were true, it is difficult to see how we could have evidence of this sort. For consider. The evidence we ordinarily appeal to in order to justify personal identity judgments—observed spatiotemporal continuity, physical or psychological similarities, and the like—could be good evidence for personal identity only if one of the following conditions obtained: (a) such facts have been discovered to be regularly connected with the presence of personal identity, (b) there is a legitimate, nondemonstrative inference from facts of these kinds to the presence of personal identity that does not rest on such observed correlations, (c) personal identity reduces to the presence of some fact or cluster of facts of the sort in question, or (d) there is some nonanalytic, a priori connection between some fact or cluster of facts of the sort in question and the presence of personal identity. But none of these conditions could plausibly be thought to hold, given the truth of the natural view.

How, on this supposition, could one establish the requisite correlations? To do so, one would have to be able to establish that personal identity holds in particular cases, independent of an appeal to any of our ordinary empirical criteria. But how could this be done? No one, after all, can check to see if all the properties a has at some time t are had by b at t and conversely, for every time at which either exists. Moreover, the idea is equally unpromising that one might be able to make a legitimate, nondemonstrative inference to the presence of personal identity from facts of the kind we ordinarily appeal to that did not appeal to such observed correlations. Presumably such an inference would be an inference to the best explanation. But there is no reason, given the natural view, to think that the presence of personal identity in any way explains empirical facts of the relevant sort. How, for example, could the fact that a relation like R (that is, a relation with the features the natural view ascribes to R) holds between a at t_i and b at t_j provide any explanation at all of the fact that a's body is spatiotemporally continuous with b's or that b's psychological features are, in large part, explainable by reference to a's? Third, the natural view rules out the possibility of a deductive inference to the presence of personal identity from empirical facts of the kinds we ordinarily appeal to by denying that any analysis of personal identity by reference to facts of these kinds is possible. And, finally, the last possibility is unsatisfactory because it simply makes a mystery of the supposed connection between the relevant empirical facts and the presence of personal identity. In other words, once we rule out the possibility that personal identity reduces to the presence of empirical facts of the kind we normally cite in evidence of personal identity, it is hard to see how there could be any a priori connection between such facts and the presence of personal identity. It would seem, then, that the natural view flies in the face of our firm convictions that we do sometimes know that personal identity judgments are true, and furthermore know such things on the basis of observed spatiotemporal continuity, physical or psychological similarities, and the like.

By adapting a line of thought suggested by Derek Parfit,[1] we can develop this objection along somewhat different lines. Consider a case of double half-brain transplantation, in which each half of someone's brain is transplanted into a different skull. Call the donor a and the postoperative persons, each of whom has a half of a's brain, b and c. (We are assuming, contrary to fact, that each half of a person's brain is causally sufficient for all of the person in question's psychological functions.) In a case like this, one of three possibilities must be realized: (1) either a is one of the resultant persons, b and c, (2) a is neither b nor c, or (3) a is both b and c. Now suppose that the relation of personal identity has the features the natural view ascribes to it. Then a can't be both b and c, for then b would be the same person as c, given R's transitivity and symmetry, and every feature b has at time t, c has also at t, for every t at which either exists. So in a case of the kind in question, a would have to be the same person as just one of b and c or he would have to be identical with neither. But if the latter were the case, it is difficult to see how personal identity could plausibly be thought to be preserved in a nonlingering single half-brain transplant case, that is, a case in which half of the donor's brain is successfully transplanted and the donor's body ceases to function during the operation. But if personal identity could not plausibly be thought to be preserved in this type of case, it's also difficult to see how it could plausibly be thought to be preserved in a full transplant case, or indeed even in a full head transplant case. But if it is doubtful that personal identity is preserved in cases of these kinds, how could it fail to be doubtful that it is preserved in ordinary, everyday cases where we normally think ourselves fully justified in ascribing personal identity? On the other hand, if we suppose that a is identical with one of b and c, we find ourselves similarly led to doubt that we are justified in making the everyday personal identity judgments we do. For if we are justified in making the personal identity judgments we do in ordinary, everyday cases, it must be because there is a connection between the empirical facts we rely on in making such judgments and the presence of personal identity. But if it could be true in a Parfit-type double half-brain transplant case that a is the same person as b (say), but not the same person as c, then a person who exists at t_j (b) can be identical with some person who exists at t_i (a), even though another person who exists at t_j (c) bears exactly the same empirical relations to the earlier individual a that b does. But this possibility implies that, in certain cases at least, the presence of personal identity has no connection at all with the kinds of empirical phenomena we ordinarily rely on in making personal identity judgments. In view of this, we can hardly feel confident that the empirical facts we rely on in ordinary, everyday cases in making such judgments do not lead us astray. After all, if personal identity can be present in one case and absent in another, when the empirical facts are the same in both, what is it about the empirical facts that hold in ordinary cases that makes it legitimate to base personal identity claims upon them?

II

The above objection to the natural view makes attractive the idea that, intuitions to the contrary notwithstanding, the relation that we judge to hold when we make personal identity judgments must be definable in empirical terms after all. More specifically, the thought becomes almost irresistible that since the relation in question must be of such a kind that satisfaction of our ordinary empirical criteria for answering personal identity questions provides us with good reasons for thinking it holds, it must be reducible to some empirical connection(s) for the presence of which things like observed spatiotemporal continuity, physical and psychological similarities, and the like can plausibly serve as evidence.

Once this thought has taken hold, a consideration of the judgments we are inclined to make in a variety of imaginable cases, together with the requirement defined by acceptance of the idea that our ordinary evidence for personal identity is good evidence, makes views like the following one tempting. Person a who exists at t_i is identical with (or the same person as) person b who exists at t_j ("aRb" for short) just in case the following conditions are met:

1. b is a "continuer" of a, where this means that b's properties "grow out of" or are causally produced by a's, or are to be explained by a's having earlier had the properties s/he then had.

2. b is a closer continuer of a than any thing else that (actually) exists at t_j; in short, b is the closest continuer of a (at t_j).

3. b is a sufficiently close continuer of a, where the properties, dimensions, and the weights they receive, which determine the measure of closeness, are functions of the kind of thing a person is.

4. a is the closest predecessor of b, that is, nothing else in existence at t_i (c, say) is such that b more closely continues c than it does a.

5. b decisively beats out the competition among any continuers of a that happen to exist; that is, b is enough closer to a than any other competitor to win decisively the "title" of being a in a later phase of a's existence.[2]

It's easy to see why such an analysis might strike one as plausible once one begins to think about the relation personal identity judgments involve along the present lines. First, if the relation is understood in this way, it is clear that the evidence we ordinarily take as showing that personal identity judgments are true will count as good evidence. The fine-grained physical similarities of b and a typically correlate with, and indeed are grounded in, b's being a continuer of a—indeed *the* continuer of a. The same is true of psychological similarities, including similarities in memory-dispositions. Observed spatiotemporal continuity is normally excellent evidence of the kinds of causal connections built into the notion of "being a continuer of." Characteristically, when b is the continuer of a, any plausible conception of what the condition of "sufficient closeness" requires will be met, and so on.

In addition, an analysis of this sort appears to match our intuitive judgments about which person is *a* in a later phase of *a*'s history in a large range of cases—both actual and imaginary. Suppose the world were such that each half of a human brain were causally sufficient for all of the psychological functions of its owner. Now imagine a case in which half of *a*'s brain is transplanted into the head of *b*, whose brain, ravaged by disease, has just been removed. Call the resulting person *c*. Imagine also that *a*'s body continues to live after the operation, although with a half-brain that is incapable of generating conscious states, whereas *c* is perfectly healthy and, when he regains conscious-ness, psychologically identical with *a* as *a* was prior to the operation. I think it would be plausible to believe that *c* is *a*, and that the body that is spatiotemporally continuous with the body that *a* possessed prior to the operation is no longer the body *a* possesses after the operation. And this is just the result that an analysis like the one in question yields—at least if, as seems plausible, the notion of a person with which we operate is one that gives greater weight to psychological continuity than to bodily continuity in determining the "measure of closeness." On the other hand, if it should happen after you die that, as a result of "a very improbable random event . . . elsewhere in the universe . . . molecules come together precisely in the configuration of your brain and a very similar (but healthier) body, exhibiting complete psychological similarity to you,"[3] we would *not* hold that you had, by chance, undergone a "secular" resurrection. And again, this is the result that an analysis like the one in question gives, since in this case the "accidental" person is not one of your continuers.

Much more might be said along the above lines to make such an analysis attractive. But since my primary purpose is to bring out some of the problems that beset both it and all approaches of the general kind of which it is an instance, I turn instead to the latter task.

Consider, to begin, so-called "beaming" cases. These are cases in which long-distance or especially swift travel (allegedly) is caused by beaming a "fully informative description of the body" of some person to a distant place, "where the body is then reconstituted (from numer-ically distinct molecules) according to the received information."[4] Now, if we construe what sufficient closeness for persons consists in, in a natural way, then a closest continuer theory like the above entails that *b*—the newly reconstituted person at the distant spot—is the same person as *a*—the one who stepped into the information-extracting and -transmitting device moments earlier—if *a* is disintegrated in the proc-ess of information extraction. On the other hand, the theory entails that *b* is *not a* if *a* is unaffected by the device and walks away unscathed after the information concerning his body has been extracted and transmitted. If this is so, then it would seem that whether b is responsible for the monstrous murders a has committed depends on such facts as whether or not a is killed by the falling safe that hits him as he walks away from the machine or has a fatal heart attack moments after the transaction, as long as the accident or heart attack occurs *before* b is synthesized. But this consequence of such a closest continuer theory is highly counterintuitive.

Moreover, should two individuals, b and c, be synthesized at the same time in accordance with the information that has been transmitted about a and if a is disintegrated in the process, neither individual is a, according to the theory in question, since although both count as continuers of a, even sufficiently close continuers, neither is, *ex hypothesi*, closer than the other, and hence neither is a's closest continuer. But this result again implies consequences that are quite unpalatable, it seems to me. For it implies that b is responsible for a's crimes if the synthesizer building c malfunctions with the result that c doesn't get built, but not if there is no malfunction. Further, if we suppose the synthesizing device to work sequentially, it implies that whichever of b and c is built first gets to bear responsibility for a's crimes, even though neither would if, owing to the development of a nonsequential, multiple copier, they had instead been synthesized simultaneously.

In addition to difficulties such as these that arise for a closest continuer analysis, there are several problems that beset a wide range of views of the same general kind, that is, analyses that appeal to just the sorts of relations—like spatiotemporal continuity, psychological similarity, and causal dependence—that are used in closest continuer analyses to define the notion of some person who exists at one time being a close continuer of a person who exists at some earlier time.[5] One of these problems is posed by the consideration mentioned above that makes the empirical unanalyzability claim of the natural view attractive: it seems intelligible that a person should die and rot away and yet at some much later point come into existence again—at the general resurrection, perhaps—despite the absence of spatiotemporal continuity, psychological similarity, causal dependence, and so forth. For if this is intelligible, then it cannot be a conceptual truth, a truth about the concept of personal identity, that personal identity holds only provided some relation or constellation of relations of the foregoing sorts obtains.

A second and parallel problem arises in connection with the impli-

cation of such analyses that whenever the appropriate relation or
relation-complex holds, there is personal identity. For again, on at
least many such analyses it seems not unintelligible that there should
be cases in which the analysans relation holds even though personal
identity fails, or anyhow whether cross-temporal identity is preserved
is at least an open question. Sufficing to make the point is the kind of
situation Austin Duncan-Jones imagined a number of years ago in his
paper "Man's Mortality,"[6] a situation in which organisms like us
possess unlimited powers of part/organ rejuvenation but a capacity to
remember that reaches back only a few thousand years. In such cases,
any or all of the empirical relations we ordinarily cite in evidence of
personal identity could well obtain between any pair of persons occupying adjacent places in the spatiotemporally continuous path between
a (at t_i) and b (at t_j), even though it is at least an open question whether
a and b are the same person, provided t_i and t_j are sufficiently far apart
and the psychological and physical features of a and b sufficiently
different. Consider, for example, the case in which b is a youthful-
appearing, athletic nincompoop, while a was a decrepit, erudite genius,
and there are no ties of memory connecting b and a.

In addition, analyses of the kind in question have the counterintuitive
consequence that there is no reason why a person should care in a
special way or degree about the existence and well-being of his future
self, provided he has reason—perhaps *per impossible*—to believe that
another will exist who is just as likely as he is to realize his most
important (non-ego-involving) goals or ends (those of his most important goals or ends the realization of which does not entail his own
continued existence). To see this, suppose we consider an analysis that
makes use only of the notion of something's being a continuer of some
earlier existent. Then, if a person did have reason to be concerned in a
special way or degree about the existence and well-being of his future
self even under the conditions indicated—namely, that somewhere
there is what John Perry has called a "metaphysical imposter" who is
as likely as he is to realize his most important (non-ego-involving)
goals or ends, and the person in question has excellent reason to
believe that this is so—it would be because he has reason to be
concerned in a special way or degree about the existence and well-
being of his continuer(s), independently of any reason to think their
existence is necessary for the realization of his most important (non-
ego-involving) goals or ends. But it is hard to see that anyone could
have reason to be concerned in a special way or degree about the
existence and well-being of his continuers, independent of reason to

think their existence is necessary for the realization of his most important (non-ego-involving) goals or ends. However, it seems clear that this fact poses a problem for advocates of views of the kind in question, because it is obvious that not only do we have reason to be concerned in a special way or degree about the existence and well-being of our future selves, but we would also continue to be in this condition even were we in the "metaphysical imposter" situation, that is, even if we had excellent reason to believe that someone else will exist in the future who is just as likely to realize our most important (non-ego-involving) goals or ends as we are.[7]

Finally, analyses of the sort in question usually—or anyway frequently—entail (a) that personal identity comes in degrees, (b) that there can be borderline cases of personal identity, and (c) that personal identity is not a one-one relation. For relations such as psychological similarity, psychological continuity, being a continuer of (in Nozick's sense), and even spatiotemporal continuity (on some natural explications) admit of degrees, are vague in the sense of allowing borderline cases, and fail to be one-one. But such entailments also fly in the face of powerful intuitions, as was noted above in the course of detailing the attractions of the natural view.

III

The upshot of the preceding discussion is that both the natural view and its empiricist alternatives are open to serious objections. To resolve the problem this situation raises, two strategies suggest themselves. One might, on the one hand, attempt to revise one or other of the empiricist analyses that populate the literature on this subject in such a way as to obviate problems of the sort detailed in the preceding section. One might, in other words, try to develop a satisfactory account of the relation in question by adding a sufficient number of epicycles to one of the recently proffered empiricist analyses to handle the objections to which it is liable. On the other hand, one might seek to resolve the problems the foregoing considerations generate by trying to develop further the natural view in such a way as to make it more palatable. Since I have little hope for success along the former path, I shall in what follows pursue the latter—although, as will be seen, I shall not succeed in constructing an account that is wholly free of difficulties.

Because the natural view rests upon what I take to be quite firm intuitions, the most plausible way of making it more satisfactory is by adding features to it rather than by modifying or eliminating any of the features defining it. Reflection suggests, I submit, that the most satisfactory view results when the natural view is revised so as to consist of the following theses. First are the theses that define the natural view as formulated above, which, it will be recalled, were these:

1. The relation that we judge to obtain when we make personal identity judgments—R—is an equivalence relation (a relation that is transitive, symmetrical, and reflexive) and hence a one-one relation.

2. R is an "all-or-nothing" relation.

3. R is neither "vague" nor "open-textured," and

4. R is "unanalyzable" in the sense that (a) no analysis can be given that appeals to such empirical relations as spatiotemporal continuity, being a continuer of, psychological similarity, and the like, and (b) no reductive (non-circular) analysis of any kind can be given.

Second are the following additional theses:

5. Empirical criteria exist for determining when R does and does not obtain, and knowledge that these criterial conditions are met (or hold) are frequently taken to justify a claim to know the truth of some personal identity judgment.

6. Persons are normally able quite confidently to make first-person personal identity judgments in the absence of any observations of the kind that are typically taken to ground third-person judgments, or indeed without the use of or appeal to criteria of any kind. Moreover, they typically take themselves to know the truth of personal identity judgments made in this way.

7. Normally, third-person personal identity judgments based upon the empirical criteria mentioned in (5) above agree with the first-person personal identity judgments that are confidently made without appeal to criteria.

8. Cases are conceivable to which these criteria are inapplicable, and cases are also conceivable in which satisfaction of these criteria leaves questions of personal identity unsettled.

(The term 'criteria' here refers to conditions whose presence or satis-faction is taken in ordinary life to constitute good reason for judging a proposition of a certain kind to be true or most probably true.)

The four additional theses—(5)–(8)—are not only quite plausible, but they clearly help to make this "revised view" (as I shall call it) more attractive than its truncated forerunner. That there exist criteria in the sense indicated for settling ordinary personal identity questions is, of course, obvious. And so also are the propositions that (a) we frequently take the evidence we have for the truth of personal identity judgments as sufficient to justify knowledge-claims; that (b), under normal circumstances, we can and do confidently make first-person personal identity judgments despite not having or appealing to evidence of any kind, and further typically feel justified in claiming to know that the judgments we make in these cases are true; and that (c) such first-person personal identity judgments do not generally conflict with the judgments of others which are made on the basis of observed spatio-temporal continuity and the like. Thus, the revised view, in conse-quence of containing theses (5)–(7), has the virtue of taking into account, in a way the natural view does not, certain aspects of our epistemic practices in this area, as well as a certain fact about the congruence of personal identity judgments, which, although obvious enough upon reflection, is rarely attended to.

Moreover, in virtue of thesis (8), the revised view also explicitly recognizes the fact that, in many imaginable cases involving personal identity questions, we simply have no idea what we should say as to who is who—and this even when all the facts are given about psycho-logical similarity, spatiotemporal continuity, and so forth that can or might be discerned by observation and inference. Many of the situa-tions involving "beaming" are cases in point. Whether there is redu-plication or not, as long as a (at t_i) is disintegrated in the process of extracting the information about his body that is "beamed" elsewhere, it is not obvious that the newly constituted person is the original person. And, if it does seem obvious, consider a pair of cases, one involving a half-brain transplant with momentary lingering of the donor and the other a half-brain transplant without lingering. If one's intui-tions are at all clear here, it seems to me they will favor identifying b (at t_j) with a (at t_i) in the latter case. But then they will boggle at the lingering case. If they are not clear in the nonlingering case, then *it* will be a case of the kind we need.

The revised view thus seems not only to be an improvement on the natural view, but to rest on a good many intuitions that seem quite deep. In view of section II, we now see that there is more to be said in support of thesis (4) than we indicated when the natural view was discussed above. The wide-ranging array of difficulties that beset empirical analyses is a substantial part of the argument in support of both the natural view and its slightly more elaborate successor. Nonetheless, even the revised view is open to the same objection that, we noted earlier, afflicts the natural view. That objection was that the natural view, by virtue of the thesis that R is unanalyzable in the sense indicated, appears to make it impossible that we should really know what we all think we do know, namely, that a vast range of our personal identity judgments are correct. Thus, if the revised view is to stand, this objection, to which it is also liable, has to be shown unsound or, if not unsound, at least undamaging.

A defender of the revised view might respond in several ways to this objection. The first is suggested by some of the ideas adumbrated in Wittgenstein's later writings. In its first formulation, the objection, it might be said, rests on the assumption that there could be an a priori connection between the kinds of empirical facts that we ordinarily cite in evidence of personal identity and the truth of personal identity judgments only if R were analyzable by reference to, and hence just consisted in, the presence of some empirical fact or cluster of empirical facts of the kind in question. But this assumption is not at all obvious. For suppose that concepts like personal identity were connected with certain empirical phenomena in such a way that it is a necessary truth, knowable a priori, that whenever, or virtually whenever, the phenomena are present the concept applies (provided the surrounding circumstances are of the normal kind or in no way provide the basis for a case for doubting or denying that the concept is applicable). Then we could justifiably claim to know on empirical grounds that certain personal identity judgments are true because these grounds sanction the relevant judgments as a matter of logic, or owing to the structure of the concept of personal identity, even though the facts that make these judgments true are not reducible to (or do not consist in) the presence of the empirical phenomena that justify them. Moreover, if this line were correct, the objection in its second formulation would also cease to be compelling. For this formulation of the difficulty similarly assumes the falsity of a Wittgensteinian view of the sort just described. For consider. On this version of the objection, if *a* is one of *b* and *c,* then empirical facts of the kind we cite in justification of personal identity under normal circumstances could not justify personal identity judgments in these everyday situations, since in a certain merely logically possible double half-brain transplant case, R could hold between *b* and *a* and not between *c* and *a*, even though *b* and *c* bear the same empirical relations to *a*. But the conclusion doesn't follow if a Wittgensteinian view of the sort just described were true. For if this were so, the mere fact that under very strange circumstances (indeed so strange that they could never arise for human beings as they in fact exist) there would be no empirical grounds for choosing *b* rather than *c* as being *a* in a later stage of his history, would not obviously impugn the epistemic value of the sorts of empirical considerations we typically appeal to in ordinary cases to justify our personal identity judgments. Moreover, the argument for skepticism about ordinary cases if *a* is neither *b* nor *c* in the bizarre case also fails should such a Wittgensteinian view be correct. The thought here, it will be recalled, was that if *a* is neither *b* nor *c* in the bizarre case, then we land on a slippery slope, at the bottom of which we find ourselves unable to give any weight to empirical considerations of the kind we ordinarily rely on to justify personal identity judgments. But again it appears that if the Wittgensteinian view were correct, the slippery slope would not be there. The mere fact, if it were a fact, that *a* was neither *b* nor *c* in the bizarre case would carry no implications for the epistemic value of our usual criteria of personal identity in everyday, nonbizarre cases. It would still be true that, in circumstances of the kind that normally obtain, it is logically impossible—or anyhow necessarily the exception perhaps—that we should have evidence of personal identity of such and such kinds and that personal identity should fail.

It is not difficult to see that this way of handling the objection under consideration is unsatisfactory. The central problem lies in establishing—or even making it plausible—that the view in question is correct. How, for example, could one show that there is no possible world in which empirically discernible relations of such and such a sort hold between *a* (at t_i) and *b* (at t_j), even though '*aRb*' fails, despite the presence of the right surrounding circumstances? Or that there is no possible world containing persons in which such failures are roughly equal in frequency to the nonfailures? It is not contradictory to say "Jones has the best possible evidence for thinking that *aRb* and the surrounding circumstances provide no basis for suspecting that his evidence is misleading, but it's nonetheless possible that not-(*aRb*)" or (b) "The best possible evidence for judgments of the form $\ulcorner \alpha \text{ R } \beta \urcorner$ leads us astray in nearly half the cases."

To put the problem in a fuller way, notice that a Wittgensteinian view of the sort in question appears to make a (variant of a) justification-conditions theory of meaning and truth unavoidable. That is, if a view of this sort were correct, then what we mean when we assert propositions of the form $\ulcorner \alpha \ R \ \beta \urcorner$ (where α and β designate persons existing at different times) will have to involve—at least in part—that such and such empirical connections hold or probably hold between the persons designated by α and β, or something of the sort. After all, on such a view it is owing to the structure of the concept of personal identity that certain empirical conditions provide grounds for holding that the concept has application. But if such empirical phenomena enter into the meaning of our judgments of personal identity, how can it fail to be the case that what it will be for such a judgment to be true is—at least in part—that such empirical connections probably hold, or something of the sort? If what we mean when we assert S is that such and such is the case, clearly what it will be for S to be true is that such and such be the case. But theories of these kinds are not obviously correct; nor is it obvious how one might argue in a convincing way in their support.[8]

It may be, of course, that more can be done to make plausible a Wittgensteinian view of the kind in question than I presently see, in which case the objection might well be one that can be shown to be without force. But if not, a defender of the natural view need not abandon his stand, for a different way of responding to the objection might serve his purposes equally well. I have in mind a response that simply grants the force of the objection, but then seeks to remove its sting. Here is one form such a response might take.

The history of thought is replete with cases in which human beings erroneously thought themselves to have adequate justification for claims to know the truth of propositions of various kinds. Not so long ago many people thought they knew that the earth was stationary, that physical objects were not 99.99 percent vacuum, that there were pairs of (nonrelatively) simultaneous events, that a drop of water put on a frying pan that has been heated to several hundred degrees fahrenheit would disappear with an explosive hiss. One thinks also in this connection of the history of proofs of the parallel postulate, Christian apologetics, and the sorry spectacle of current public debate on issues like abortion. In this light, the idea that we never have adequate justification for claiming to know the truth of our personal identity judgments, despite our firm prephilosophical intuitions to the contrary, may not seem so unpalatable, after all.

This response to the objection under consideration might then be supplemented and thereby rendered a bit more compelling by a plausible account of how we might have come to be in the prima facie unlikely position of (a) making all those judgments that may, for all we know, be false; (b) making many of them on the basis of what we are convinced pre-reflectively is adequate evidence; (c) making many others on no basis whatever; and yet (d) making these too with full confidence that we do so correctly and "with right." Such an account might run thus.

It is currently accepted as established fact that our genetic material has a major role in explaining why it is that we characteristically come into the world with one heart, two eyes, and ten fingers. It is also widely accepted—and not without reason—that what goes on in our conscious experience is largely or wholly dependent upon such matters as the ways our neurons are interconnected and their patterns of firing. But if these things are so, it's easy to see how it could be true that various of the ideas we employ in thinking about ourselves and the world should be as they are owing largely to our genetic equipment, and hence to the selective advantage of having these ideas, or at least to having the genes that characteristically express themselves phenotypically—at least inter alia—in operating with such ideas. Indeed, not only could it be true that a sizable body of our conceptual baggage is "innate" in the sense of being genetically determined in much the way or sense that our gross anatomy is genetically determined, but there is a growing body of argument to this effect. I shall not here rehearse and try to evaluate this literature; suffice it to say that many of the considerations Chomsky has adduced over the years for thinking that human beings possess an innate "knowledge of universal grammar" and many of the arguments Fodor has recently elaborated in defense of a version of concept nativism are easily adapted or useable to support the view that much of what might be called "the metaphysics of common sense" is similarly innate.[9] By this expression I mean the system of concepts that includes, among others, the concepts of space, time, and mind-independent, persisting material things; the ideas of past, present, and future; the notion of causation; the idea of other minds; the notions that lie behind the distinction between the necessary and the contingent, together with the conception of an array of nonactual possible worlds to which they give rise; and the ideas of objective truth and a point of view that transcends all limited, idiosyncratically conditioned points of view, a point of view from which things are (or could at least in principle be) viewed *sub specie aeternitatis*.

With these remarks as background, it is easy to see how we might have come to be in the prima facie strange position described one paragraph back. We might simply be so constituted that we make personal identity judgments just as we do: (a) in the third-person case on the basis of certain kinds of empirical grounds; (b) in the first-person case on no basis whatever (typically); (c) in both cases confident that our judgments are by and large correct and confident also that we make them "with right," whether on the basis of empirical evidence or not; and (d) in such a way that third-person and first-person judgments about the same individuals tend to agree. Yet our idea of how a person who exists at one time is related to some person who exists at a later time when we judge that the former is the same person as the latter might not correspond to any relation that actually holds among things that exist at different times, just as our idea of a unified space, or a responsible action, or an absolutely past event, or a being that exists in all possible worlds, might not correspond to anything that is really there.

If such a possibility as I have just described were actual, the connection between the empirical facts that are criterial, in the sense indicated above, for the cross-temporal identity of persons in third-person cases and the presence of such a relation would be both nonanalytic and independent of experience. For the relation we judge to hold in personal identity cases would not be reducible to empirical phenomena of the kind we appeal to in justifying our judgments; yet it would also be true that we had not learned through experience that the phenomena we take as evidence for the presence of the relation we judge to hold in these cases does provide us with good reason to make these judgments. If the world were this way, it would be a world containing, in a sense, a nonanalytic, a priori connection between certain criterial phenomena and the facts that they (ostensibly) ground; moreover, a nonanalytic, a priori connection rooted in the truth of what perhaps not surprisingly would be a variant of Kant's transcendental idealism.

Unfortunately, even if the foregoing remarks go some way toward removing the sting of the objection to which even the prima facie, more attractive successor of the natural view is subject, it is still far from being a fully satisfactory view. Recall the Duncan-Jones fantasy adumbrated earlier. Human beings are imagined to be capable of rejuvenating their organs and other parts, with the result that human bodies typically trace very long spatiotemporal paths. But our memory capacity is limited, and our interests and values change through time. This fantasy suggests an argument against the revised view like the following. (1) If the relation R that we judge to hold when we make personal identity judgments is transitive, then a K-case is not logically possible, where a K-case is one in which (for instance) aRb, bRc, cRd, . . ., yRz, but not-aRz (or it is an open question whether aRz). (2) But such cases are possible. It's possible after all that the relation of which the revised view speaks (the relation we ordinarily judge to hold in personal identity cases) is applicable and that the criteria we ordinarily employ in personal identity cases do lead us to apply the notion correctly. It's also possible that there should be human beings who have the features indicated in Duncan-Jones's fantasy. But this entails that it's possible that there should be a case in which on January 1, 1983, a_1 is the same person as b_1 on January 2, 1983, that b_1 is the same person on January 2, 1983, as c_1 on January 3, 1983, . . ., and that $y_2 50$ on January 1, 18,000,083 is the same person as $z_2 50$ on January 2, 18,000,083, even though it's an open question whether $a_1 R z_2 50$. $z_2 50$, after all, is, we can imagine, quite youthful, handsome, interested in tennis and basketball, madly in love with Sue, intellectually undeveloped and culturally a barbarian, stupidly patriotic, and psychologically addicted to cocaine and low humor, whereas a_1 is quite aged, bald and warty, a Nobel Prize–winning physicist, possessed of wide-ranging intellectual culture, quite devoid of sexual or romantic impulses, cosmopolitan, sophisticated, but quite humorless. Moreover, $z_2 50$ has no recollection of any of the events in a_1's life or of any events before the year 16,500,001 C.E. (3) Hence, it is false that the relation that we judge to hold in cross-temporal personal identity cases is transitive, and so false that the theory in question—the revised view—is correct.

IV

It was suggested at the outset that personal identity judgments are among the most puzzling we make, that they are a source of deep perplexity. I trust that the discussion above has at least indicated some of the main considerations behind this claim. In view of this discussion, one might even be tempted to conclude that the topic of personal identity, perhaps as much as any topic in philosophy, simply reveals— in Hume's words—"the whimsical condition of mankind."[10] A less pessimistic and perhaps more sober conclusion would be that we should seek to content ourselves with the least unsatisfactory view, all things considered, recognizing that in philosophy, as in life itself, the best or optimal may fall considerably short of the ideal. Yet another conclusion would be that our ways of thinking about the problem of approach that is orthogonal to the ones that have heretofore filled the literature: not more epicycles, but a conceptual analogue of the Copernican Revolution.

It is difficult, I submit, not to feel at least some sympathy for all three of these conclusions. Still, the first strikes me as unnecessarily defeatist, and the third, insufficiently realistic. I thus take the second to be the most plausible conclusion, all things considered, and accordingly view the last-mentioned difficulty with the revised view as one of the costs involved in embracing it—the cost of denying, perhaps somewhat counterintuitively, that K-cases are in fact logically possible.

Notes

1. See D. Parfit, "Personal Identity," *Philosophical Review* 80 (January 1971): p. 4 f.
2. The view stated in this paragraph is similar to "the (local) closest continuer theory" presented by Robert Nozick in *Philosophical Explanations* (Cambridge: Harvard University Press, 1981), chap. 1. It differs mainly in treating personal identity in the way Nozick treats object identity through time; that is, it makes the measure of closeness a function solely of the kind of thing a person is, rather than partly a function of the person in question's decision.
3. Ibid., p. 41.
4. Ibid. Nozick also considers under this heading cases in which the molecules of the decomposed body are beamed to the distant place and there reassembled.
5. Here I have in mind analyses like those suggested recently by Sydney Shoemaker in "Identity, Properties, and Causality," in Peter A. French, Theodore E. Uehling, Jr., and Howard K. Wettstein, eds., *Midwest Studies in Philosophy,* Vol. 4: *Studies in Metaphysics* (Minneapolis: University of Minnesota Press, 1979); John Perry in "The Importance of Being Identical," in A. Rorty, ed., *The Identities of Persons* (Berkeley: University of California Press, 1976); and Derek Parfit, "Personal Identity."
6. See Austin Duncan-Jones, "Man's Mortality," *Analysis* 28 (January 1968).
7. The general line of thought in this paragraph obviously owes much to Perry's discussion in "The Importance of Being Identical," despite running counter to its general tenor.
8. The issues involved here are treated in Chapter 8.
9. See, for example, Noam Chomsky, *Rules and Representations* (New York: Columbia University Press, 1980): and Jerry Fodor, *RePresentations*

(Cambridge: MIT Press, 1981), especially chap. 10 ("The Present Status of the Innateness Controversy").

10. David Hume, *Enquiry Concerning Human Understanding,* sec. XII, part II (last paragraph).

CHAPTER TWO

Freedom, Necessity, and Chance

Consider next remarks like "He did it all right, but he certainly could have refrained from doing it," and "She's going to perform that action, but she certainly has it within her power not to do it." Such remarks are common in everyday speech, and a certain idea they express—the idea of being able to refrain from doing (or having done) something one will do (or has done)—readily gives rise to puzzlement. In this chapter, I shall again trace several of many possible paths of reflection to bring into relief some of the considerations that make this idea so perplexing. As I proceed, various ways of resolving the problems this idea generates will be indicated and their costs underscored.

I

If a thin wire is inserted into a certain part of a human brain and an electric current is passed through it, certain bodily movements will take place. Electrical stimulation of other parts of the brain will give rise to experiences of specific kinds—visual, memory, and so on.[1] Findings of this kind, together with much else that we know about the structure and functions of the human brain, make it quite plausible to think that all the bodily movements involved in the kind of behavior we normally think of as, in some sense, within a person's control are a result of neural occurrences within the person's brain. Assuming that this is so, imagine that a group of aliens from a highly developed civilization in some other part of the galaxy have studied us for several years from afar, and now have it within their power to affect the neural occurrences within our brains, without our knowledge, and to predict in detail exactly what bodily movements particular neural interventions will effect. Imagine further that all the bodily movements involved in all the intentional behavior of some human being—call him "Kermit"—during the last year have been brought about by the intervention of these aliens, who have in consequence been able to predict all his movements in advance of their occurrence. Apprised of these circumstances, we would be strongly inclined to deny that Kermit could have done other than what he did during the year. And we would doubtless absolve him from responsibility for any crimes he may have then committed, refuse to give him credit for any saintly deeds he may then have performed, and so forth.

Now erase the aliens and their supertechnology from the picture. Imagine instead that each neural occurrence they caused in Kermit's brain during the year in question was brought about by some immediately preceding state of affairs or condition, which was in turn brought about by some immediately preceding state of affairs or condition, and so on back to some time before Kermit's birth. Here I am imagining that each of the states of affairs or conditions in question "had to occur" or was "necessitated" once the condition causing it obtained, in the same way or sense in which an ordinary window pane in ordinary circumstances has to break when a large rock is hurled against it, when the water in a glass has to become ice when placed in a properly functioning freezer under normal circumstances, and when a cube of butter has to melt when, in normal, everyday circumstances, it is placed in a hot frying pan. If this latter picture were to have application, what was said above about Kermit would also be true in these somewhat altered circumstances. Again, it seems plausible to hold that Kermit could not have done other than what he did during the year. Again, were we convinced that the circumstances described held, many of us would doubtless insist that he deserved neither praise for his good behavior nor blame for his bad. And what would be true of Kermit under the envisaged circumstances would be true of anyone under sufficiently similar circumstances. In a world where all our bodily movements are necessitated in the way certain of Kermit's are, *ex hypothesi,* we like him would be puppets in the hands of forces beyond our control. Or so, at any rate, it is easy at first blush to feel.

Moreover, the scenario does not seem much changed if the neurological events that give rise to the bodily movements involved in some stretch of behavior are (a) "spontaneous" (or "chance") occurrences in the sense in which, according to current physical theory, the radioactive decay of an atom of rhubidium is spontaneous (or due to chance), or perhaps (b) expressions (or manifestations) of such "un-caused" occurrences at the subatomic level. Altering the picture in this way does nothing, on the face of it, to restore the power to have done otherwise. All it does is to ensure that these bodily movements, or some of them, occur "out of the blue," so to speak. But the fact that Raskolnikoff's crashing his axe into the head of the pawnbroker's sister was due to a chance occurrence at the subatomic level—or a collection of such occurrences—and so happened "out of the blue," in no way helps to restore his power to have done otherwise, or to ensure the appropriateness of holding him responsible for his action.

Let 'BM-determinism' stand for the thesis that every bodily move-ment involved in a piece of human behavior is "chain-necessitated," that is, necessitated by some immediately preceding event or state of affairs, which in turn is necessitated by some immediately preceding event or state of affairs, and so on back to a time before the agent in question came into existence. (Here 'necessitated' is explained by appeal to examples of the breaking, freezing and melting kinds indi-cated above.) Let 'BM-indeterminism' stand for the thesis that at least some bodily movements involved in human behavior occur owing, in part, to "chance" occurrences—perhaps at the subatomic level—and those that do not are "chain-necessitated" in the above sense. And let 'FW' stand for the doctrine that human beings possess free will, where this is understood to mean just that it is true of at least some of our behavior that we could have refrained from engaging in it. Using these abbreviations, we can summarize the thesis the foregoing considera-tions make plausible: if either BM-determinism or BM-indeterminism is true, FW is false. Or if FW is true, then both BM-determinism and BM-indeterminism are false. I shall refer to this thesis as "the incom-patibilist thesis" or simply as "incompatibilism."[2]

II

The incompatibilist thesis does not, of course, say anything about whether BM-determinism, BM-indeterminism, or FW is true. What it does do, if true, is to place a certain constraint on attempts to elucidate what is involved in FW, that is, what is involved in a course of behavior's being within our power to engage in or not engage in. In particular, the thesis requires that FW be understood in such a way that its truth entails the falsity of BM-determinism and BM-indetermin-ism, and that the truth of either of these theses entails the falsity of

FW. In this and the following section, I shall set forth and indicate the problems with versions of two prominent, alternative ways of understanding what FW involves that purport to satisfy this constraint. I shall speak of them respectively as "the *causa sui* view" and "the *sui generis* view."

A person has it within his power both to do and not do a certain action A, according to the *causa sui* view, just in case (1) his decision (or volition) to do (or not do) A (a) is not caused by any immediately preceding condition or state of affairs, and (b) is caused by the decision (or volition) itself, *or* (2) his decision (or volition) to do (or not do) A, although not necessitated by any preceding condition or state of affairs, expresses a (nonbinding) commitment to a general policy of action the original decision for which satisfies (a) and (b) above. This account of what FW involves clearly requires a good deal of elucidation. I turn next to this task.

The word 'decision' in this account can be understood to pick out a certain kind of mental occurrence, in particular a mental event of accepting a certain reason for doing an act as decisive or a mental event that consists in assigning weights to various considerations for and against performing an act in such a way that one side prevails. "Volitions" are understood here as exercises of the will, meaning by this simply acts of choosing to do (or not do) certain actions. ('The will' in this use would be just another label for the power or capacity by virtue of which a being not only can engage in action but could have refrained from doing some of the things the being in fact does.) I shall take it as presupposed by the account as given that decisions of the relevant sort (or exercises of the will) necessarily give rise to the actions or omissions in question, that is, causally determine those actions or omissions. The sense of 'cause' in (a) of (1) above (and in the presupposition just mentioned) is that employed earlier and elucidated by appeal to examples. But in clause (b) of (1), the notion of causality involved is a different one. Here the relevant idea is that a decision causes itself when it consists in (or anyhow involves) accepting a principle (or general policy) to the effect that all the agent's decisions should exhibit such and such a feature and the decision to accept this principle (or to do, or not do, an act that involves acceptance of this principle) exhibits the feature in question. (I will soon give an example of a decision that causes itself in this sense.) In this use of 'cause' (and its cognates), x is the cause of y provided the occurrence of y can be explained in a certain way by appeal to x. (I shall hereafter use 'cause$_n$' to refer to the sense of causality involved in (1)(a) and 'cause$_{cs}$' to refer to the sense involved in (1)(b).) Last, what is involved in a decision's expressing a nonbinding commitment to a general policy of action is simply that its occurrence has been rendered more probable than any other in virtue of the occurrence of the previous decision to follow that policy, where the occurrence of an event is more probable than the occurrence of any alternative of the relevant kind in the sense, whatever it is, in which it is more probable that an electron should be found in this region than in that should we make the relevant observations.[3]

It is evident why this account of what FW involves satisfies—at least ostensibly—the constraint imposed by the incompatibilist thesis. If BM-determinism were true, the bodily movements a given action involves will have been necessitated by conditions or states of affairs that obtained before the agent's birth. But if this were so, then a decision to do the action in question would have either to be irrelevant to whether the action takes place or to be caused$_n$, that is, be a (noninitiating) link in the causal chain that leads to the bodily movements the action involves. In either case, it would not satisfy the conditions FW involves on the account in question.

Moreover, this is also the case if BM-indeterminism should be true. For in this event, either (i) all of the bodily movements a given action involves are chain-necessitated, or (ii) some of the bodily movements this action involves are chance occurrences or (iii) some are necessitated by a causal chain initiated by some chance event or states of affairs. If (i) is true, then the action will fail to be free for the reasons just indicated. If, on the other hand, (ii) or (iii) holds, the bodily movements in question will not be caused by a decision to do the action in question, or will be caused by a decision that either is caused$_n$ or is a purely chance phenomenon, that is, a phenomenon that is neither caused$_{cs}$ nor rendered more probable than otherwise by a previous caused$_{cs}$ decision. Whichever of these possibilities holds, FW as understood by the account in question will not be true.

Unfortunately, this account of what FW involves is open to a number of serious objections. First, it is not obvious that FW is an intelligible doctrine, so understood. It does seem that there could be decisions that, in some sense, cause certain actions to be performed and that satisfy conditions (a) and (b) of clause (1). At any rate, the idea of an event that is not necessitated by preceding states of affairs is not, on the face of it, incoherent. And it is easy to construct plausible examples of possible decisions that are reflexive in the required sense. A decision to make only decisions that have the effect, so far as one can tell, of maximizing the amount of existing intrinsic value is a case in point. For such a decision might well be a decision that exhibits the feature in question, that is, it might be a decision that has the effect, so far as one can tell, of maximizing the amount of existing intrinsic value. Moreover, we can perhaps make sense of the idea that a decision of the above sort should render future decisions of a certain kind more probable in the requisite sense. But how we should understand the idea of a decision to perform an action that involves the acceptance of a general policy of action as well is not clear, assuming that the idea is distinct from the idea of a decision that establishes a tendency to make decisions of a certain kind thereafter.

This problem could perhaps be remedied by a minor alteration of the account. The second difficulty is less superficial. In brief it is that, appearances to the contrary notwithstanding, the account does not really satisfy the incompatibilist constraint. Again, it's true that there is a difference between chance occurrences of the kind involved in radioactive decay and the uncaused$_n$ decision that FW on the present account involves—at least if we focus on reflexive decisions to accept general policies. The former lack the kind of explanation of which the latter are susceptible. But such reflexive decisions nonetheless are very like those paradigm chance occurrences, since for any given reflexive decision, another could have occurred in its place, all facts about the history of the world up to that point remaining the same. Insofar as this is the case, there is clearly an important sense in which there just is no explanation of why that decision occurred rather than some alternative.[4] Moreover, the sense in which there is an explanation of such a reflexive decision is Pickwickian at best. The mere fact that a decision of mine has the features that the principle decided upon by that decision requires of all my decisions hardly provides a basis for saying that that decision is thereby explained in anything like the way a person's strong desire to do A explains his doing A, or the absence of oxygen in most of the building explains why the fire did not spread. In the latter cases, we understand why he did A or the fire didn't spread. In the former case, we don't understand why that decision, rather than some other, was made. Needless to say, the nonreflexive decisions that occur in consequence of the reflexive one inherit this inexplicability, with the result that they too are more like the paradigm chance occurrences than might at first appear.

A third objection to the present account of what FW involves is that it fails to square with our ordinary understanding of when it is correct to say of someone that she could have done otherwise or that he had it within his power at t both to do and to refrain from doing A. Consider, for example, James Whitman, the young man who several years ago climbed to the top of a tower on the University of Texas campus and began to shoot at passersby below. Suppose that following the autopsy, he had been discovered to have had a large brain tumor that put pressure on parts of his brain in a way that is known empirically to give rise to extremely aggressive behavior. In a case like this, we would normally be quite doubtful about whether he could have controlled his aggressive impulses and whether he could have refrained from doing something of the general kind he did in fact do. But now if the account in question were correct, it is difficult to see that such doubt would be justifiable or appropriate. There are, after all, no empirical data correlating the presence of such tumors or impulses and the absence of uncaused$_n$ decisions, or uncaused$_n$ decisions expressing tendencies established by reflexive uncaused$_n$ decisions. So if the account in question were correct, then it is entirely possible that his decision to murder as many innocent people as he could in the way described was not caused$_n$ by the states of affairs that preceded it, whether it was a reflexive decision or one expressing a tendency set up by such a decision. Moreover, the only "explanation" possible for his decision, in this case, would be, or would involve, one of the Pickwickian explanations provided by a reflexive decision. And if all of this is so, it is hard to see what possible role his brain tumor could play in justifying or making appropriate a doubt of the kind in question.

Finally, there is the objection that, if this account were correct, it is hard to see how we could have any reasons to think that FW is true. We don't, after all, have any reason to think that there are any uncaused$_n$ decisions or any reflexive decisions that establish tendencies for subsequent uncaused$_n$ decisions to follow a certain pattern. Yet we would need to have such reason if we were to have a basis for thinking that anyone could do other than what he in fact does do, as this notion is understood on the present view. But it's hard to believe that we never have any justification for thinking what we all do think, that sometimes it is true of us that we could have refrained from doing what we did.

III

I turn now to the second of the two ways of understanding what FW involves that putatively satisfies the incompatibilist constraint. On the *sui generis* view, as I have labeled it, the power possessed by human beings both to do and refrain from doing a certain action is "a power to initiate causal chains"—in particular, causal chains that lead to movements in some part or parts of the agent's body, where agent A *initiates causal chain C* just in case the first member of C—*e*, say—(a) is not causally necessitated by a preceding event or state of affairs, (b) occurs or obtains because A brought it about or made it happen, and (c) this simply by virtue of A's having "willed" or chosen or executed an intention that *e* occur or obtain, or that some event or state of affairs occur or obtain that has as a (causally) necessary condition that *e* occur or obtain. Given (a) it follows that the willing or choosing or intention-executing referred to in (c) is not to be thought of as an event that causes$_n$ the occurrence or obtaining of *e*. Furthermore, on this view, the relation that holds between an agent A and an event or state of affairs *e*, when A initiates a causal chain that begins with *e*, is a *sui generis* causal relation. Put in a slightly different form, on the *sui generis* view, the truth of FW involves the truth of the following propositions.

1. At least some events or states of affairs are not caused$_n$ by any preceding events or states of affairs.

2. At least some of these uncaused$_n$ events or states of affairs include physical events of the sort that are the causally sufficient conditions[5] of various bodily events such as neurological occurrences inside people's brains—and perhaps also mental events such as decisions, flights of fancy, acts of recollection, and the like.

3. At least some of the latter are caused by the agents whose bodies or minds these events or states of affairs involve, and this through their simply "willing" (choosing, executing an intention) that, for example, their arms move, certain mental images appear, a certain decision be made, or certain words come out of their mouths.

4. The causal relation—hereafter "causes$_{sg}$"—that sometimes holds between an agent and an event or state of affairs that begins a causal$_n$ chain is one that is not susceptible of a reductive analysis.[6]

The argument that this view satisfies the incompatibilist constraint is straightforward and obvious. Suppose that FW is true and that the account correctly explicates what its truth involves. Then both BM-determinism and BM-indeterminism will be clearly false, the former because some of the bodily movements of a human being are not chain-necessitated, and the latter because at least some of these bodily movements that are not chain-necessitated are not chance occurrences either, since they arise because of events or states of affairs that the agent causes$_{sg}$.

Like its predecessor, this view is open to a number of serious objections of a similar kind. The first can be put thus. If the *sui generis* view is intelligible (that is, if the theses that this view involves constitute a collection of propositions that logically could all be true), then there are possible worlds in which they *are* all true. Let one such world be called w_1. But if w_1 exists, surely there is also a possible world w_2 that is just like w_1, except that in w_2 there is no causation$_{sg}$. Rather, the brain events that in w_1 are caused$_{sg}$ by the agents whose heads house the brains in question are just chance occurrences in w_2. But since w_2 is like w_1 in every other respect, the "willings" (choices, and so forth) that occur in w_1 through or via which the agents there cause$_{sg}$ certain brain events to occur also occur in w_2, although in w_2 they are, so to speak, wheels that do not engage the rest of the mechanism. Also as in w_1, the people in w_2 believe that they are responsible for various of their bodily movements; however, in w_2 these beliefs are all illusions, whereas in w_1 they are (by and large) true. At any rate, it is difficult to see why w_2 would not be among the possible worlds if w_1 is. However, this objection continues, it is far from clear that there are possible worlds that differ only as w_1 and w_2 do. If we were in w_1, there would be no way of ever discovering by empirical investigation that we were not in w_2 instead. In other words, there seem to be no empirical differences between w_1 and w_2. But it seems that the proposition that there is causation$_{sg}$ is the sort of proposition that, if true, could in principle be known true. Yet if this proposition is true, it does not seem on the face of it to be a truth that is knowable a priori. So it must be knowable empirically, if knowable at all. It follows that it is at least problematic that the *sui generis* view is intelligible.

The central idea behind this objection leads directly to a second, even stronger objection. The advocate of the *sui generis* view, according to this objection, is caught in a dilemma. For given that w_2 is possible if w_1 is, he has to concede (a) that his view is unintelligible or (b) that there is no way of discovering by empirical means whether FW is true, on his understanding of what it involves. But neither consequence is very attractive. He clearly has to reject the former, but the latter is also quite unpalatable. For clearly, we do think we know that people sometimes were able to abstain from actions they in fact performed. Yet he has to hold, if he sticks to the *sui generis* view, that such putative knowledge is either a priori or impossible. But it is not at all plausible, as I have said above, to think that we know a priori that there is such a thing as causation$_{sg}$. Hence, the advocate of the *sui generis* view, it would seem, has to deny the firm commonsense conviction that we do sometimes know of a person that he (or she) had it within his power not to have done something he did do.

Another way of putting what is essentially the same objection is this. If we become convinced by empirical evidence that whenever a person takes a certain amount of a drug, she does whatever she can to kill or maim all those she thereafter encounters until the drug wears off, then we would be very doubtful whether A, who has just taken the requisite dosage, could have behaved sweetly to the man who asked her for directions. But an advocate of the *sui generis* view would have to deny that this attitude was reasonable. For, since the existence of the power to initiate causal chains is not an empirical matter, on his view, there could be no empirical evidence that would justify doubts as to whether a person could have behaved differently than she did. But if this is right, then the *sui generis* view does not give expression to the idea we normally have in mind when we assert FW.

IV

In view of the foregoing discussion, it is clear why the locutions with which we began are so problematic. The puzzling situation at which we have arrived can be summed up as follows. It is a firm conviction of common sense that we are able, at least sometimes, both to do and to refrain from doing certain things—in short, that FW is true. Reflection suggests, however, that the incompatibilist thesis is also true; in other words, that the truth of FW is incompatible with both BM-determinism and BM-indeterminism. Yet there does not seem to be any way of reconciling these ostensible truths. For there are only two *prima facie* viable candidates for ways of understanding what FW involves that satisfy the incompatibilist constraint, and both are open to serious objections.

It would seem, then, that unless ways can be found of meeting these last objections or some different way of conceiving FW discovered that both satisfies the incompatibilist constraint and is objection-free, we must either reject the incompatibilist thesis or deny that human beings ever have it within their power to do anything other than what they do do. In the present section, I shall consider what can be said in behalf of the first of these last two ways of resolving the problem.

A variety of considerations might be advanced against the incompatibilist thesis. Among the more central of these are the following. It is clear, a defender of this way of resolving the problem might begin, that we do sometimes have it within our power both to do a certain action and to refrain from doing it; in other words, FW is obviously true. But it is equally clear that, as regards the bodily movements our actions characteristically involve, there is no intelligible alternative to the view that either BM-determinism is true or BM-indeterminism is true. In other words, these two theses are not only mutually exclusive but also exhaustive of the possibilities. For suppose BM-determinism is false. Then either certain bodily movements would either be uncaused$_n$ or be the result of (relatively short) causal chains, the first members of which are uncaused$_n$. But if this were so, then these bodily movements would fail to be chance occurrences or the more or less immediate outcomes of chance occurrences only if these occurrences were explainable, and explainable in some way other than by citing either events that necessitate their occurrence or by appealing to an inherent propensity for things of that kind to occur under certain circumstances. But no other way of explaining such occurrences is conceivable. If this is so, however, then the truth of FW does not involve anything that is ruled out by the truth of BM-determinism or BM-indeterminism, appearances to the contrary notwithstanding. Hence, the problem under consideration is rooted in illusion.

This line of thought could be supplemented and strengthened, of course, by appeal to some of the difficulties (noted in the preceding sections) that beset the attempts to articulate an understanding of FW that satisfies the incompatibilist constraint. For they can be viewed as attempts to provide an understanding of a different type of explanation of certain bodily movements than those available in a world where BM-determinism or BM-indeterminism holds sway. But even when thus supplemented and strengthened, this line of thought is less than satisfactory, and this in three respects. First, it does nothing to explain how the illusion it allegedly exposes comes to possess us. Second, its premise to the effect that BM-determinism and BM-indeterminism exhaust the possibilities is not, I submit, at all compelling, as the continuing power of the *sui generis* view to attract followers makes evident. And third, it provides no clue as to what the truth of FW involves given, as it claims, that one or the other of BM-determinism or BM-indeterminism must hold.

A second and quite different argument against incompatibilism avoids both the second and third of the above difficulties. It begins with the intuitively plausible claim that the evidence we accept in everyday life in support of judgments such as "He could have done something different" and "She had it within her power to refrain from doing what she did" is good evidence—indeed, sufficiently good upon occasion to support claims to know that judgments of these kinds are true. This fact, the argument then continues, would not hold unless it were the case that what the truth of FW involves is just that sometimes what a person does is not done in ignorance, or under coercion, or as a result of brain manipulation, and so forth; and it is done by someone who has reached "the age of reason" and is not otherwise incompetent owing to senility, psychosis, neurotic trends or other debilitating states. For consider. The evidence we accept in everyday life as good evidence for saying of someone who has just begun a vigorous exercise program that she could have refrained from taking this drastic step is such facts as (a) she was not forced to begin the program by a threat to life or limb, (b) she did not begin it as a result of receiving a posthypnotic suggestion, (c) she was not suffering from a delusion that moving her limbs in certain ways was necessary to warding off the evil influence of demons or witches, (d) she was not suffering from a condition that led her to feel intense anxiety when not engaged in certain kinds of exercise, and so forth. But if these kinds of considerations justify us in feeling confident, or even claiming to know, that so and so could have done otherwise than she did, how could it fail to be the case that what we're judging when we judge true a proposition of this kind is just that facts of the above sort hold. We've certainly not discovered any correlation between the holding of such facts and some further, empirically hidden "power" resident in the human soul. If it were empirically hidden, how could we? And there is surely no basis for thinking that an inference to the best explanation is involved here— an inference to the existence of a nonempirical "power" as the best explanation of facts of the sort we take to be evidence that a person could have done otherwise on some occasion.

But now, the argument concludes, if the preceding considerations are correct, it follows that what FW involves is that sometimes facts of the kind just indicated hold in connection with the exercise program example, and hence that the truth of FW is quite compatible with both BM-determinism and BM-indeterminism, since facts of the kind in question could hold on specific occasions if either of these doctrines were true.

Despite this argument's avoidance of two of the difficulties mentioned in connection with the first line of thought presented, because it does not avoid the first the argument appears open to reversal. Why, someone might say, isn't it simply a mistake to judge that the person mentioned above could have refrained from starting the exercise program, even if she is free of psychotic delusion, neurotic compulsions, and so on, and even if she is in full command of her faculties, uncoerced, and so on. If either BM-determinism or BM-indeterminism is true, the bodily movements her behavior involves will have been chain-necessitated by events or states of affairs that go back in time beyond her birth, or they will be the result of chance occurrences over which she has no control and for which she is no way responsible. In either case, it is difficult to see how her behavior could be correctly described as behavior that she could have refrained from engaging in.

V

In the absence of a compelling account of why the argument for incompatibilism fails, a solution to the problem posed by the discussion in sections I through III that rests upon a rejection of incompatibilism will not be very satisfactory. If that is so, to deny the truth of FW appears to be the only way out.

Unfortunately, this way of resolving the problem is, on the face of it, at least equally unsatisfactory. It is hard to find firmer intuitions than those that lie behind our conviction that we do sometimes have it within our power to refrain from acting as we do. And it may well be, in addition, that a vast range of the emotions and attitudes that pervade our lives derive their viability from the truth of FW. Would indignation ever be justifiable if FW were false? Would resentment? Would it ever be appropriate to forgive another if what she had done she could not have failed to do? Could we ever feel justifiable respect for ourselves or others in a world where FW failed?

Whatever the correct anwers to these last questions, the cost of solving the problem at hand by denying FW will be considerable. Still, a solution along these lines is not without its attractions. The difficulty with the attempts to reconcile incompatibilism and FW are severe, and the argumentation in support of incompatibilism, quite powerful. In addition, it is easy to construct a plausible account of how we might have come to possess the intuitions that underlie FW that does not require their truth. The account runs parallel to that toward the end of Chapter I, sec. III. Here is how it might go.

It is a widely acknowledged fact that what happens in our minds is in some sense a "reflection" of neural structures and transactions.

Furthermore, much at least of what is involved in the way our nervous systems work is genetically based. These facts suggest that it is at least possible that various of the "ideas" that pervade everyday thought and discourse are rooted in the genome, in the sense that we naturally come to operate with this conceptual equipment in the normal course of our intellectual development, at least as long as the environmental inputs to which we are subject in the course of development are within a certain normal range. Moreover, if this story were correct, there would be reason to think these ideas matched the world only if there were reason to think the genes or gene clusters underlying them would not have become part of the human gene pool unless the convictions that were their phenotypic expressions were true. But it is at least plausible to think in the case of many of the ideas that might be genetically based that this is not so. Many ideas might confer a selective advantage, whether true or not. And in any case, genes can contribute to the presence of many phenotypic features, only some of which confer a selective advantage on their possessors. Thus, it is at least possible that we should be constituted so as to operate with a notion of "the will" that gives rise to our intuitive convictions that FW holds, and nonetheless that this conviction is false.

Moreover, if such a story were true, it is easy to see how it might also seem both that the incompatibilist thesis is true and that FW and incompatibilism are irreconcilable. Thus, the notion of "the will" that is native to us might well be such as to make the standard argument for incompatibilism attractive. In addition, this notion might come with certain empirical criteria of application of just the sort we in fact employ in deciding when a person could have done otherwise, which would explain why both the *sui generis* and the *causa sui* accounts of what FW involves appear objectionable.

Despite its attractions, however, solving the problem at hand by rejecting FW is, for the reasons noted, far from an ideal way out of the darkness that has traditionally characterized this area of metaphysics. Whether it represents a more attractive way than its alternatives, as I am at present inclined to believe, each reader will judge for him- or herself.

Notes

1. See, for example, Dean Wooldridge, *The Machinery of the Brain* (New York: McGraw-Hill, 1963), p. 163; Richard L. Gregory, *Eye and Brain* (New

York: McGraw-Hill, 1966), p. 68; and John C. Eccles, *The Human Mystery* (London: Routledge & Kegan Paul, 1984), p. 204 f.

2. This use of 'incompatibilism' differs only slightly from its common use by philosophers who have written in this area.

3. I have drawn the *causa sui* view essentially from the account Robert Nozick provides in *Philosophical Explanations* (Cambridge: Harvard University Press, 1981), chap. 4, although it is also similar in important respects to a view Paul Grice sketched in a lecture at the University of Washington in the autumn of 1981.

4. Nozick, it should be noted, does recognize this problem. See *Philosophical Explanations,* pp. 300 ff.

5. Or, anyhow, causally sufficient when taken together with the circumstances in which they occur.

6. I have drawn this view essentially from the account Roderick Chisholm develops and defends in "Freedom and Action," in K. Lehrer, ed., *Freedom and Determinism* (New York: Random House, 1966).

CHAPTER THREE

Materialism and the Mental

I

Many human beings are strongly inclined to seek some kind of understanding of the world, or reality, as a whole. The result of this inclination is the historic development of a plethora of so-called "world views." A long-standing and currently attractive world view is the materialistic (or physicalist) view. Although materialism has been given a number of somewhat different detailed articulations since the time of Leucippus and Democritus, one way of putting briefly the central conviction of many of its proponents would be as follows: everything that ever exists—or at least every concrete object—is composed solely of matter, and every event or process that ever takes place consists solely of interactions among material things.[1] Such an account remains quite obscure, of course, in the absence of some elucidation of the notions of matter and material things. For present purposes, it will suffice to say that the objects postulated by current theories of the atom, the nucleus, and the elementary particles, as well as their scientific successors, together with all the objects or stuffs solely composed of such things—presumably, water, carbon, alcohol, gold, proteins, cellulose, bone, blood, and so forth—count as matter or material things.

It is not difficult to see why materialism, so understood, is widely attractive to those who yearn to "see things whole." To begin, the work of physicists over the last few hundred years has resulted in a body of theory concerning atoms and their constituents that is as well-confirmed as any theory we have; and it takes a good deal of subtle philosophical argumentation to make persons who understand the theory and its evidential warrant even slightly doubtful about whether there is good reason to believe that the entities the theory ostensibly refers to really exist. Second, given the conviction that such entities exist, the evidence that the things and stuffs we perceive around us and that populate "the natural order"—water, trees, rocks, glass, living creatures, stars, galaxies, and so on—are solely composed of atoms and the elementary particles constituting them appears increasingly overwhelming. And third, there is simply no basis for thinking there exist (occur) any nonmaterial things (or events) "outside" the natural order that is generally accepted by those in a position to understand and evaluate the relevant considerations. Arguments for the existence of one or more immaterial "gods," in a realm beyond or above the natural order, for example, lack the ability to create conviction in unprejudiced minds. Moreover, the same is true of arguments designed to make plausible the claims that some body of literature, person, or collection of events is a "revelation" of such a god or gods.

Despite materialism's attractiveness, however, a certain cluster of considerations has made it seem obviously false to many reflective people. I shall first set out the main considerations in this cluster; then, in the rest of the chapter, I shall develop one of a number of possible ways in which the obstacle these considerations pose for the materialist might be overcome.

II

When one reflects on the idea of a material object—at least when such objects are at or above the molecular level—such propositions as the following seem to be true, and even necessarily true.

1. Such objects are "spatially located" at any moment of their existence. No sense can be made of the thought that a certain molecule of gold, for example, exists at some time, and yet that it is not then situated anywhere in space.

2. Such objects are "public" in the sense that no one is in an epistemically privileged position as regards the existence or nature of any such object—at any rate, no one is in such a position as a matter of necessity. A person might as a matter of contingent fact be in a better position than anyone else at *t* to know of the existence of some rock, say, but it seems never to be a necessary truth that some person should be in such a situation vis-à-vis any material object. Anything

that one person can know about any material object can, in principle, also be known by other persons.

3. Such objects are "objective" in the sense that whatever can be known about them by creatures with perceptual mechanisms and intellectual dispositions of such and such a kind can also be known, at least in principle, by creatures who are constituted quite differently, as long as the latter are sufficiently sophisticated perceptually and intellectually to be capable of doing mathematics and physics at the levels of the first group. That is, it seems obvious upon reflection that facts about the existence and natures of things like atoms and anything solely composed of atoms are accessible to any creatures capable of observation and sufficiently sophisticated theorizing, whatever the peculiarities of their modes of perceptual interaction with the world and however idiosyncratic (to us) their ways of intellectually processing the data their observation of the world yields.

4. Such objects are "awareness-independent" in the sense that their existence does not require (necessitate) the existence of any conscious being (or beings) to apprehend them. In other words, any atom or item solely composed of atoms can exist even though unperceived.

5. Such objects are "not essentially conscious or self-conscious." That is to say, for any such object, there is a possible world in which that object exists but is never at any point during its career either a conscious being (that is, characterized by beliefs, desires, perceptual experiences and the like) or a self-conscious being (that is, characterized by such n-order conscious states [$n > 1$] as the desire that it have such and such first-order desires, the awareness that it is undergoing such and such emotions, the belief that it intends to create such and such beliefs in others, and so forth). Moreover, its never being conscious or self-conscious in the possible world in question is not owing to the fact that its normal course of development has been aborted.

6. Such objects "lack intentionality" in the sense that they neither "possess content" nor are "directed upon objects" in the way in which, for example, beliefs, dreams, and perceptual states "possess content," and desires, emotions like fear and love, and certain kinds of thought are "directed upon objects." That something solely made up of atoms should have propositional content in the way my belief that the moon is devoid of life has, or should be directed at an object in the way my fear of flying is, appears on the face of it quite senseless.

Moreover, identical or analogous truths appear to hold of all events and processes that consist solely of interactions among material things.

They, too, for example, are of necessity localizable (at least roughly), public, objective, and awareness-independent. They, too, it would seem, are not essentially characterizable in mental terms. And any instance of C-fiber firing, it seems, could occur in another possible world and not have the features that are essential to something's being an experience of pain or a case of someone's having an after-image. And they, too, appear to lack intentionality, and necessarily so. No such events or processes, one naturally thinks, are directed to objects or possess content in the way or sense in which emotions like fear and love are directed to objects and attitudes like hope and expectation possess content.

Given the intuitive attractiveness of points like the foregoing, it is easy to see why the materialist world view has struck so many as inadequate.

1. It has struck many as not only false but as even without clear sense to speak of a visual hallucination or a feeling of deep depression as being located just behind the bridge of one's nose or just above one's liver. And, furthermore, to many it has even seemed not obviously inconceivable that the world should have contained all of the experiences that human beings ever have—perceptual, emotional, intellectual, and so forth—even though nothing was spatially located anywhere, nor was there such a thing as space. So it seems to be false that experiences are located in space—and indeed a necessary fact about them that they are not.

2. It has also seemed obvious upon reflection that not everything that exists or occurs is "public." For each of us is in a position to know that he is having the pains and itches he is and what his current memory-images and thoughts are images and thoughts of in a way that is different from, and more certain than, any way others have of knowing such things about us. Moreover, this does not seem to be so owing to a relation to these facts that holds contingently and that another might have had to them instead. The apparent reason why these things are so is just that my knowledge that I am now in pain, for example, is immediate, that is, not mediated by my knowledge of anything else, such as facts about my body—and necessarily so; whereas your knowledge that I am now in pain is not similarly immediate—and necessarily so. And similarly for my knowledge and your knowledge of what my current thoughts and memory-images are thoughts about or images of.

3. Yet a third line of thought against materialism turns on the kind

of objectivity everything would seem to possess if materialism were true. When we reflect on dolphins and their peculiar modes of communication, the sonar perceptual mechanisms of bats, and various more bizarre possibilities that may be actualized in creatures who have evolved under very different planetary conditions, the conclusion is almost irresistible that no matter how sophisticated our grasp of the neurophysiological facts concerning these creatures and the way they interact with their environments, as long as we are not built along analogous lines, we shall simply not be in a position to understand what it is like to have experiences of the kinds they have.[2] In other words, the conclusion is almost irresistible that the subjective character of the experiences such beings have will be hidden from us, however complete our scientific knowledge of the inner workings of these creatures and their causal interactions with the surrounding world. But if this conclusion is correct, it seems to follow that not everything that exists or occurs is objective in the sense indicated above. So if everything would be objective in this sense were materialism true, materialism evidently fails.

4. Then there is the fact that many of the things that exist are apparently "awareness-dependent." Consider, for example, an onslaught of intense back pain or a sudden thought that the thermostat has not been turned down for the night. Surely neither of these episodes could take place without the person (or animal) who undergoes them being aware that he has come to be in pain or to have the thought in question. Yet if materialism were true, nothing, it would seem, would be awareness-dependent in this sense.

5. Reflection also suggests, and again contra materialism, that some among the items that really exist are essentially both conscious and even self-conscious. Consider oneself, for example. If one were not essentially conscious, then there is a possible world in which one exists and yet is not conscious at any point during one's history in that world, and this not merely because one's normal development has been thwarted. There one is, perhaps, a rock or a volcano or a typewriter. But surely it is no more possible that you should have been a rock instead of a conscious being than that you should have been the number 7 or Beethoven's Fifth Symphony. You undoubtedly could have been different from what you are in lots of ways; you could have been taller, smarter, a frequent visitor to Rio, and so forth. But there are limits, we intuitively feel, and the line separating conscious from nonconscious beings, hazy as it may be, clearly defines one of them. Moreover, it is not at all implausible to suggest that the line separating

self-conscious from nonself-conscious beings—in the sense of this expression given above—defines another.

6. Finally, there is the apparent difficulty for the materialist that stems from the intentionality of the mental, that is, the fact already mentioned that certain mental phenomena, such as occurrent thoughts of various kinds, beliefs, hopes, wishes, certain emotional and perceptual states, and desires "possess content": (in some sense) take objects, propositional or otherwise, or (in some sense) are about or refer to things other than themselves. Thus the thought I am now having that Sam will be late tonight is about Sam; something about it carries a reference to a certain person who is distinct from the person having the thought. My hope that one day there will be universal nuclear disarmament somehow involves the proposition that there will someday be universal nuclear disarmament. And my fear of flying is, in some sense, directed upon the "object": travel by airplane. Yet, as noted above, the truth of materialism appears on the face of it to be incompatible with the existence of phenomena like these.

III

I turn next to a line of thought that might be advanced to overcome objections, of the kinds just sketched, to materialism. Let us note, to begin, that mental phenomena can be divided into two broad classes. On the one hand are those phenomena that ostensibly consist in the relation of a subject to a proposition: the so-called propositional attitudes. These include believing, desiring, hoping, expecting, wishing, and so on. On the other hand are the phenomena that are not so characterizable. If the term 'sensation' is used to cover the "data" of both bodily perception—the pains, itches, tingles, feelings of nausea, heart palpitations, and so forth—and the experiences that (typically) result from the exercise of the so-called organs of sense—visual, auditory, olfactory, and gustatory experiences, sensations of pressure, heat, and wetness, and so forth—then it is plausible to maintain that all the phenomena in this latter class are either "sensations" or are analyzable by reference to some constellation of propositional attitudes and sensations. In any case, it should be clear that if a materialist can handle the problems posed by both the propositional attitudes and sensations, he will at least be well on the way toward a materialist account of all mental phenomena.

The objections to materialism that stem from the phenomena that fall under the rubric "sensations" are, as we have seen, based upon certain beliefs that have considerable intuitive plausibility. One way a materialist might meet these objections would be along the following lines. Consider the belief that the visual experience I am now having is ineluctably nonobjective in the sense indicated above. What is such a belief about? Well, it's about a certain "object," viz., the "object" believed to have the property of non-objectivity. But how should we understand what the phrase following 'viz.' refers to? There appear to be two equally correct ways of answering this question. On the one hand, this phrase, it seems, refers to whatever counts as the proximate cause of my belief that I am now having or undergoing a visual experience, that is, the "object" that immediately gives rise to this belief. Why, after all, does the belief in question exist? How did I come to have it? Clearly, in a case of the kind in question—a belief about a sensation I am currently having—because the occurrence of the "sensation" has caused it. On the other hand, it is plausible to think that the phrase also refers to whatever, if anything, has the properties the various beliefs immediately generated by the former "object" imply the sensation in question has. For convenience of reference, I shall call the former the "external object" of this belief and the latter its "internal object," since the latter's nature, but not the former's, is logically derivable from the beliefs the former causes.

With this distinction at hand, the materialist might then suggest that although the property of nonobjectivity may well belong to the internal object of the belief in question, it does not obviously belong to its external object, since what characteristics the latter has is a scientific question and hence not one that can be settled merely by a priori consideration of our doxastic states. So whether the belief in question gives rise to an objection to materialism depends upon the answer to two questions: (a) Does its external object possess the property of nonobjectivity? and (b) Does its internal object exist; that is, does there exist anything in the real world that corresponds to, or has all the properties of, its internal object? But, he might then argue, the answer to (a) is plausibly "No," since the only properties we can expect to find by doing empirical investigations into the causes of such mental phenomena as beliefs are physical ones. And the answer to (b) certainly could well also be "No"; at any rate, we certainly do not know that it is not. Moreover, any independent reasons we have for thinking materialism true—such as philosophical difficulties with non-materialist views—will provide a good basis for thinking it is "No."

Finally, the materialist could go on to suggest that exactly parallel considerations can be deployed in connection with all the other objections sketched above so far as they can be based upon the existence of sensations. That is, a distinction can be drawn between the external and internal objects of, for example, my belief that this after-image is not spatially located, my belief that this itch is private, my belief that this experience of nausea is awareness-dependent, my belief that this pain is essentially abhorrent, and my belief that this memory-image is an image of my mother. Then it could be noted that the properties in question belong of necessity only to the beliefs' internal objects, that it is not at all obvious that anything in reality corresponds to *these* objects, and that empirical investigations into the nature of their external objects will only yield properties compatible with the truth of materialism.[3]

This line of defense rests, or course, on the possibility that the internal and external objects of a belief of the kind in question can fail to be identical. For if they are necessarily identical, then the fact that the internal object must possess the properties it is believed to have ensures that the cause of these beliefs—the external object—will also possess them, and hence the possibility that sensations should both exist and fail to be nonobjective dissolves. The materialist, however, can buttress the suggestion that these objects can fail to be identical by reminding us of the many cases in which sincere reports have been given by people whose knowledge of their native tongues is unquestionable, to the effect that some sensation (or sensations) they are currently having (or recently had) possess no noncontradictory descriptions. Thus, one of Köhler's subjects in the inverting spectrum experiments reported seeing two heads at the same time, both right side up and upside down. Similar reports are to be found in the literature on drug-induced states, abnormal psychology, and religious mysticism. These cases, of course, demand that the external and internal objects of the beliefs in question be distinguished, since no real object, event, or process can be correctly characterized by a contradictory description. Once our attention has been drawn to cases like these in which the nonidentity of internal and external objects is demanded, our conviction that they always must be the same dissolves. And once we concede that they need not always be identical, room has been made for the materialist thought that they may well always diverge.[4]

The objections to materialism that are rooted in the existence of the propositional attitudes might be dealt with in an analogous way. All we need is an account that is at least plausible and that is not known to be false, according to which, although the propositional attitudes—such as beliefs, and desire—do possess various of the problem-engendering features, nothing that really exists, that enters into the causal network of the world, does. Such an account is not far to seek. The following is one such account.

The beliefs, desires, and so on that we ascribe to human beings and (with limits) to certain nonhuman animals are features of theories that we construct and employ for purposes of interpreting and predicting behavior. Restricting ourselves to just beliefs and desires, such theories take the form of (more or less) holistic accounts of the belief-desire structures of the minds of the target organisms in question that are built up by asking such questions as the following: (a) What beliefs would such an organism have, given its perceptual capacities, its cognitive needs, and its stimulus history? (b) What desires would it have, given its biological needs, the means available to it for satisfying them, its likely beliefs in view of its history, perceptual capacities, and cognitive needs? (c) What systems of beliefs and desires would make its behavior—including its verbal behavior (if any)—rational? Each belief and desire posited is then construed (roughly) as a disposition to behave in certain ways under certain circumstances, namely, in ways it is rational to behave, given the other beliefs and desires posited as well. What underlies the use of such schemes, of course, is the fact that the matter of which such organisms are made, and the ways it is put together in them, are such that schemes of this sort do in fact lead to (more-or-less) correct predictions of behavior in a large range of cases. For all that, however, the posited attitudes are not causally efficacious entities that operate in the real world. Only the material objects of which such organisms are made, and the events and processes their interactions involve, are real in this sense. The belief-desire theories we employ are mere calculational devices, so to speak, and the mental states they posit have the same status as those that might be ascribed to a chess-playing computer in the course of trying to determine its most likely next move.[5]

To be sure, the organisms in relation to which such belief-desire theories might be predictively useful may well be structured in such a way that there is a close similarity between the material processes that underlie and cause their behavior and the mental structures posited in our belief-desire theories of them. Indeed, there might even be material structures in their brains that line up belief-by-belief and desire-by-desire with the beliefs and desires our theories ascribe to them, although such a close isomorphism does not seem to be a necessary condition of the existence of organisms relatively to which such belief-desire theories are predictively useful. But however this may be, it would not follow that such material structures had all the features possessed by the propositional attitudes these belief-desire theories involve. Indeed, it does follow that they would not, insofar as such attitudes are conceived in such a way as to possess properties that raise difficulties for materialism.

An organism's beliefs, for example, are evidently conceived as lacking a determinate location in space. Thus, if a man's belief that his wife is blond were spatially located in his head, and his head were in the oven, it would follow that his belief was in the oven. But clearly the inference fails. But this fact about beliefs does not raise a problem for materialism if the present story is correct. For beliefs, on this story, do not exist as elements in the causal network of the world. And the same point can be made in connection with the various other features of the propositional attitudes that ostensibly pose problems for materialism.

Among the possible objections to an account like the foregoing are the following: first, it might be objected that if beliefs and other propositional attitudes are "unreal" in the sense that this account involves, then it is hard to see why they are conceived as they are, a problem which, it might then be suggested, does not arise on the traditional model according to which beliefs, desires, and the like are viewed as immediate objects of mental vision. On this traditional model, such items are conceived as they are because they are immediately perceived to have the properties built into the relevant concepts. Second, it might be objected that the account in question overlooks the fact that we self-ascribe beliefs and desires in addition to ascribing them to others, an omission which, when rectified, has fatal consequences for the account. For once we reflect upon the fact in question, the idea that beliefs, desires, and the like might be "unreal" (in the requisite sense) appears preposterous. When we focus on the third-person case, the thought that the beliefs and desires we ascribe might have no more "reality" than the beliefs and desires we might ascribe to a chess-playing computer can at least gain a foothold in our minds; but once we shift our gaze to our own current beliefs and desires, the situation changes. Then it becomes quite impossible to think of such items as elements in a mere calculational device, useful in predicting behavior but devoid of ontological import. Third, there is the objection that the view the account in question involves of our basis for ascribing beliefs and desires in third-person cases makes a mystery of the fact that first- and third-person ascriptions tend to agree. After all, it might be said, we clearly do not ascribe beliefs and desires to ourselves on the basis of a more-or-less holistic theory constituted by asking such questions as what system of beliefs and desires would make our own behavior rational. Such theorizing is—for the most part—clearly unnecessary in the first-person case. But if this is so, then what could possibly explain the congruence of first- and third-person ascriptions if the account in question were correct?

These objections, however, are by no means fatal. As regards the first and third, a proponent of the account in question might again appeal to the fact that we are constituted as we are. More specifically, he might say that perhaps the different propositional attitudes are conceived as they are because, at least in part, operating with notions of belief and desire and the like that encapsulate the features these notions do—for example, nonlocalizability—is native to the species. Of course, some of the features exhibited by propositional attitudes will have other sources. The "privacy" of beliefs, for example, will derive from the disposition we all have to self-ascribe beliefs confidently, correctly, and "with right" independently of observation or inference—a disposition that is part of our native equipment. And a proponent of the account in question might say that what explains the (rough) congruence of first- and third-person ascriptions of beliefs, desires, and the like is the disposition just noted that accounts for the noninferential character of first-person ascriptions, taken in conjunction with the fact that third-person ascriptions rely to a large extent upon the verbal behavior in which such a disposition characteristically manifests itself among language-using animals. Moreover, the second objection might be met by making a distinction parallel to the one drawn above in connection with sensations. Consider my second-order belief *b* that I believe that the moon is a large rock. This belief that I have such and such a belief can plausibly be held to have both an external object and an internal object: the former will be *b*'s proximate neurophysiological cause; the latter, whatever (if anything) has the properties the beliefs generated by *b*'s external object imply my belief about the moon has. With this distinction in mind, it might be said, the objection loses its force. For once again, given the possibility of a divergence of external and internal objects, the possibility that nothing in the real world corresponds to *b*'s internal object seems not at all implausible. Moreover, what can be said of the moon-belief can also be said of every belief, including of course belief *b* itself.

IV

My aim in the preceding section has not been to show that materialism is true. Rather, I have sought only to suggest that the materialist is not without resources for meeting various of the prima facie objections posed by certain alleged facts about minds and mental phenomena. Moreover, it should be noted that the materialist response I have developed to such objections is by no means the only one, or perhaps even the most powerful one. The literature in this area also contains quite plausible materialist accounts of sensation that do not rely on the external-internal distinction, and equally plausible materialist accounts of the propositional attitudes that do not exempt them from causal roles in the explanation of behavior.[6] However, I hope that enough has been said to suggest that in this area also, it may well be that the world is not quite what it may at first blush seem, and that it could indeed be quite different from the way it is pictured by the commonsense scheme we tend to embrace before our innocence has been eaten away by the acids of critical reflection.

Notes

1. This is the account that Richard Boyd gives in "Materialism Without Reductionism: What Physicalism Does Not Entail," in Ned Block, ed., *Readings in Philosophy of Psychology,* vol. 1 (Cambridge: Harvard University Press, 1980), p. 85.

2. This particular objection to physicalism has been persuasively stated by Thomas Nagel. See his *Mortal Questions* (Cambridge: Cambridge University Press, 1979), p. 12, and *The View from Nowhere* (New York: Oxford University Press, 1986), chap. 2.

3. This line of defense derives, in an obvious way, from Daniel Dennett's essay "Two Approaches to Mental Images" in *Brainstorms* (Montgomery, Vt.: Bradford Books, 1978).

4. The central idea of this paragraph is set out in Daniel Dennett, "On the Absence of Phenomenology," in D. Gustavson and B. Tapscott, eds., *Body, Mind, and Method* (Dordrecht: D. Reidel, 1979). The material on the inverting spectacle experiments is alluded to on p. 110.

5. Something close to this line of thought is found in various places in Daniel Dennett's writings. See, for example, *Brainstorms,* passim; "Three Kinds of Intentional Psychology," in R. Healey, ed., *Reductionism, Time and Reality* (Cambridge: Cambridge University Press, 1981); "True Believers: The Intentional Strategy and Why It Works," in A. F. Heath, ed., *Scientific Explanation* (Oxford: Oxford University Press, 1981); and "Making Sense of Ourselves," *Philosophical Topics* 12 (Spring 1981).

6. On sensations, see Paul Churchland, "Functionalism, Qualia, and Intentionality," *Philosophical Topics* 12 (Spring 1981); and Sydney Shoemaker,

"The Inverted Spectrum," *Journal of Philsophy* 79 (July 1982). On propositional attitudes, see William Lycan, "Form, Function, and Feel," *Journal of Philosophy* 78 (January 1981); and Sydney Shoemaker, "Varieties of Functionalism," *Philosophical Topics* 12 (Spring 1981).

CHAPTER FOUR

The Possible and the Actual

I

Another notion that finds frequent expression in everyday thought and speech is the notion of situations that could have developed, but didn't, or states of affairs that might have obtained, but don't. Thus, we commonly say such things as "The Sonics could have performed better than they did on Tuesday evening," meaning: the situation in which they did perform better could have come about; and "He might have caught her cold yesterday," meaning: the state of affairs that consists in his catching it is one that might have obtained (been realized). Situations that don't develop but could have (or didn't develop, but might have) are sometimes called "counterfactual situations." States of affairs that might obtain but don't (or might have been realized, but didn't get realized) are sometimes called "possible but nonactual states of the world." From this notion of counterfactual situations, or possible but nonactual states of the world, the route to the idea of possible worlds is direct and seemingly quite unproblematic. Suppose that some situation that didn't develop, but could have, really had developed; or suppose that some state of affairs that might obtain, but doesn't, really did hold. For example, suppose that I had been two inches taller on my thirtieth birthday than I in fact was, or that you die in an automobile accident on the Labor Day weekend of 1999 rather than in the way you in fact will die, by accidental poisoning next year, let us suppose. In either case, the facts that make up reality as it is—past, present, and future—would be different in some way or ways. But this is just to say that a different world would have been actual from the one that is: a world would have been actual that contains, for example, the fact that I am two inches taller on my thirtieth birthday than I in fact was. A "nonactual possible world" so-called is just such a world. Moreover, since there are countless ways in which reality might have been different from the way it in fact is, there seem to be countless nonactual possible worlds. And since the actual world also delineates (or articulates) one of the ways the world might have been different had one of these nonactual worlds constituted the real world, it too counts as one of the possible worlds.

Now this conception of an array of possible worlds one of which is actual also yields a good many perplexities once we begin to reflect upon it. This chapter and the next will be devoted to laying out a number of these.

II

Suppose we ask ourselves what distinguishes the actual world from the other (nonactual) possible worlds. Two replies seem quite natural. The first and perhaps most obvious is that the actual world is "actual" and the other possible worlds are not—they are "merely possible." This reply is not at all helpful. For one thing, it leads immediately to a slightly altered version of the original question. Now one wants to ask, "And what is it for a possible world to possess (or lack) actuality?" Or "What does the actuality of the actual world consist in?" But this reply is also unhelpful, because lots of individuals in various nonactual possible worlds also judge that their worlds are actual. It's possible that yesterday at noon I should have had the thought, "This world differs from the others by virtue of being alone actual," although in fact I had no such thought. So there is a possible world in which I do have that thought, and refer in so thinking, one supposes, to the nonactual possible world in which that thought occurs. How does it help, then, to make clear what distinguishes the actual world from the other possible worlds to say simply that it's actual, when others in other worlds say the same of their worlds?

An ostensibly more helpful and also quite natural reply is that what distinguishes the actual world from the others is that it alone is "concrete," whereas they are "abstract entities" of some sort. Considerations like the following make this answer initially attractive. I could have painted my house green last year, although I did in fact paint it brown. Now what does the truth of the first part of this statement really amount to? Surely, it might be said, just in the fact that there is a story, although a false story, that can be told about its having been painted green last year. So the existence of a possible world in which I painted my house green last year consists in the existence of a piece of fiction, a collection of propositions at least some of which are false. Or consider the idea of a bat with the intellectual capacities of a chimpanzee. There are no such creatures— chimbatzees, we might call them—although there might have been. What does this idea amount to? A natural answer is that it simply consists in the thought of a certain complex property. But if that's right, then the judgment that there could have been such beasts is just a judgment that a certain property might have been instantiated. But this is tantamount to saying that the existence of a possible world in which there are such beasts consists only in the existence again of a certain set of propositions, one of which is the false proposition *Q has instances,* where Q is the complex property in question.

Attractive as this last reply to the question as to what distinguishes the actual world from the other possible worlds may appear, it too is problematic. In the first place, the actual world, it is very natural to think, is made up—at least in part—of things like you and me, houses, trees, planets, and galaxies. It is, in short, an entity at least some of the constituents of which are "concrete," and in that sense it is a concrete entity. But if this thought is tempting, it is surely just as tempting to think that the other possible worlds are things of the same kind. After all, they too—or many of them anyhow—contain people, houses, trees, planets, galaxies, or analogous items. And we can hardly say that such concrete inhabitants of other possible worlds don't really exist, whereas the denizens of the actual world really do; or that the states of affairs involving merely possible creatures of flesh and blood do not really obtain, whereas states of affairs like *Ronald Reagan being president in 1984* really do obtain. For assuming that the existence of chimbatzees is a genuine possibility (that there are possible worlds containing such beings), chimbatzees really do exist in those worlds in exactly the sense or way in which you and I really exist in the actual world; and various states of affairs involving chimbatzees really do obtain in those worlds in exactly the sense or way in which *Ronald Reagan being president in 1984* obtains in the actual world.

In addition, there is the following argument against the idea that the nonactual possible worlds are mere abstract entities. Let us call the entire collection of true propositions, the collection that may be thought of as representing the actual world, 'Omega'. Now suppose that nonactual possible worlds are abstract entities; suppose, for example, that each possible world is just the collection of propositions that would be true, or alternatively the collection of states of affairs that would obtain, if that possible world were actual.[1] Then Omega has the special status of alone representing (what is in part) a big, concrete particular, the particular that is the mereological sum of all the persons, plants, animals, inanimate objects, processes of digestion, volcanic eruptions, and so forth, that populate reality. (I say "in part" since the actual world may well comprise various abstract entities in addition, such as properties, relations, propositions, sets, numbers, and the like.) But now, this argument continues, the truth that Omega is special in this way is a truth that seems to hold in every possible world. Why is this? Let 'O' abbreviate the proposition that Omega is special in the way indicated. Clearly, if O is true, then it is also true that O holds in the actual world (hereafter "α"), since any true proposition is a member of Omega and holds in α. Call the proposition that O holds in α 'O*'. Obviously O* is true in every possible world. For that any proposition holds true at α is a proposition that would be true whichever of the possible worlds were actual. But there is no clear distinction between O and O*. To assert that Omega is special in a certain way—O—is not different from asserting that O holds in α—O*. The one form of words expresses the thought that the set of propositions that represents α has a certain feature f and the other expresses the thought that the set of propositions has f in α; but these thoughts are indistinguishable. Hence, if O* is a noncontingent truth—one that holds in all possible worlds—so is O. But it cannot be a necessary truth that Omega is special in the way indicated. One of the firmest intuitions in this area of metaphysics is that some of the states of affairs that actually obtain could have failed to obtain, and hence that it is a contingent matter which of the possible worlds is actual. Hence, nonactual possible worlds are not abstract entities of some kind—collections of propositions, for example. Rather, like the actual world, they are (inter alia) complexes of concrete objects that differ from the actual world not in kind, but only in what goes on at them.[2]

It will be useful to have an abbreviated version of the above argument before us for convenience of reference and ease of comprehension. Again, let 'O' abbreviate 'Omega is special by virtue of alone representing a world that is concrete', and let 'Possible worlds are abstract' abbreviate the thesis that nonactual possible worlds are abstract entities of some kind. Also, let us call the thesis that possible worlds are—at least in part—"big concrete particulars" or complexes of concrete things "the Modal Parity Thesis." Then the above argument—hereafter "the Omega Is Special Argument"—can be summarized thus:

1. If possible worlds are abstract, then O.
2. If O, then it is a necessary truth that O.
3. It is false that it is a necessary truth that O.
4. ∴ It is false that possible worlds are abstract.
5. If 4, then the Modal Parity Thesis holds.
6. ∴ The Modal Parity Thesis holds.

This argument is clearly valid. Also, its first and third premises are hard to fault: we do intuitively want to say that there is just the difference between Omega and the abstract entities that are (or represent) nonactual possible worlds that premise 1 indicates. And, as I have noted above, nothing could be clearer in this area than that it is a contingent matter which of the possible worlds is actual. Moreover, premise 5 is not a proposition that will be disputed by any who are tempted to acknowledge the existence of nonactual possible worlds in the first place. Thus, if the argument fails, it looks as though it will have to be because of a difficulty as regards premise 2.

It might be thought that the following argument poses just such a difficulty. Suppose Omega—the abstract entity that represents the actual world—is a set of propositions and that 'Beta' names a slightly different set, but one such that (a) all its members could have been true together and (b) if they had all been true, they would have completely described a possible world that would in that case have been actual. Now if premise 2 of the Omega Is Special Argument were true and O held as well, Beta would contain O, given the prima facie plausible view that necessary truths hold in every possible world. But then it would be true that if the world described by Beta had been actual instead of the world described by Omega, it would have been true even then that O. But that is clearly false: if the world Beta describes had been actual, Omega would not have alone represented a "big concrete particular." Hence either premise 2 fails or it is false that O. But O is obviously true; so premise 2 fails.

Unfortunately, this argument against premise 2 of the Omega Is Special Argument, attractive as it may at first appear, does not do the job it purports to do. For it presupposes a distinction that a defender of the Omega Is Special Argument would reject, namely, a distinction between the notion of a proposition's being true-at-such and such a possible world and the idea of a proposition's being true *simpliciter*.

The argument presupposes this distinction by making use of the latter idea in the premise that states that if the world described by Beta had been actual instead of the one Omega represents, O would even then have been true, that is, true *simpliciter* and not (just) true-at-the world described by Beta. After all, O is true-at-the world described by Beta in virtue of being a member of the set of propositions Beta comprises. Hence, if the premise in question did not employ the notion of truth *simpliciter* but the notion of truth-at-w instead, O would be true (that is, true-at-the world described by Beta) whether or not the world described by Beta were actual. Yet an advocate of the Omega Is Special Argument has to assume that all truth is truth-at-a world, and hence reject the distinction in question. This is so because his support for the second premise of this argument relies, as we have seen, on the thought that there is just no difference between O's being true-at-α and O's simply being true.

It seems then that the question that needs to be addressed is the question whether the distinction just indicated is a real one. It is easy to see that this is the same question that is posed by the earlier considerations presented in support of the Modal Parity Thesis. For if the distinction is real, then we can hold that what differentiates the actual world from the other possible worlds is that the inhabitants of the latter really exist and various states of affairs involving these existing things really obtain; for we can explicate these ideas by appeal to the truth *simpliciter* of propositions like *Ronald Reagan exists* and *Ronald Reagan is president of the U.S. in 1984,* maintaining that, for example, *Chimbatzees exist,* although true-at various possible worlds, is not true *simpliciter.* Unfortunately, powerful reason can be adduced on both sides of this question whether the distinction between truth *simpliciter* and truth-at-a world is genuine. I shall give those in support of the claim that the distinction is real in the following section. Those in support of the denial of this distinction, and *a fortiori,* in support of the soundness of the Omega Is Special Argument for the Modal Parity Thesis, are constituted by the difficulties with the conception of possible worlds as abstract entities. These are set out in the immediately following chapter.

III

Suppose all truth is truth-at-a world and that what we're saying when we say that a proposition is true without qualification is just that it is true-at-α. Then the Omega Is Special Argument will be sound and the Modal Parity Thesis true. Now consider the set of possible worlds in which I am taller than 6′3″ on my thirtieth birthday. Each of these is either a world in which I exist, or a world in which I fail to exist; that is, either it is the case that in each of these worlds there is something that is strictly and literally identical with me, or nothing in any of them is strictly and literally identical with me. (Which is the case will depend upon exactly what are the truth conditions of propositions like *RC might have been taller than 6′3″ on his thirtieth birthday.*) Suppose the former is true. Then there is a possible world *w* and a concrete "object" in *w, a* say, with which I am strictly identical and that bears no spatiotemporal relation to me and that has no causal connections with me. Worse, this object possesses properties I never have (in α), such as being 6′3″ on his thirtieth birthday. Moreover, it is hard to see that the ostensible problem posed by these facts can be dissolved by noting that though *a* has P and that I lack P, both *a* and I have P-in-w and lack P-in-α. For what is it to have a property in a possible world but to have the property and to exist in that possible world?[3] So the trouble remains that *a* and I, though strictly identical, do not share all our properties.

Also, if there is cross-world identity and the Modal Parity Thesis holds, then supposing it to be possible that I perform the most monstrous actions, there are possible worlds in which I do perform such actions. But how then can I avoid being a moral monster, and how could it be the case that I don't deserve any evil that befalls me? (Don't say, "You also reach the heights of saintliness here and there in logical space." That's surely not the correct answer, and in any case no amount of saintly behavior can make a good person of one who tortures little children for the fun of it.)

It will also be true on the assumptions indicated that if I try to make a judgment that involves reference to α, I shall be unable to succeed. Thus, suppose I judge that my death will probably occur before A.D. 2030. How could I make clear which of the possible worlds I am talking about? It won't do to say "The world I'm talking about (or have in mind) when I make the judgment in question is the world in which my death occurs," for that event—the one picked out by the phrase 'my death'—presumably occurs in many worlds if, as we are assuming, there is cross-world identity. For similar reasons it won't do to say "The world I have in mind is the one in which I exist" or "The world I have in mind is the world that contains this very judgment." For I exist in many other worlds also, and so does the judgment in question.

But if none of these ways of specifying the world I mean will do, how could it be done?[4]

Suppose, on the other hand, that there is no cross-world identity. Then we escape the above problems, but only at the price of saddling ourselves with others that are on the face of it equally serious. To begin, all of our properties become essential to us, since for any object a and any (time-indexed or omnitemporal) property P that a possesses—such as weighing 150 lbs at noon EST, June 1, 1984, or being the second son of Esther and William Coburn—there is no possible world in which a exists and lacks P. But it is clearly counterintuitive to hold that it is one of my essential properties, one of the properties that I (logically) could not fail to have, that I have on a blue shirt today. It follows, of course, that if all my time-indexed and omnitemporal properties are essential in the sense that I (logically) could not fail to have them, then all the actions that I perform are actions that I (logically) could not have failed to perform. But if fatalism (in this sense) is true, it is difficult to see how I could justly be held responsible for any of the actions I do in fact perform. It also follows from this Leibnizian essentialism that every false singular proposition is necessarily false and that every true singular proposition entails every true proposition.[5] Thus the proposition that Reagan is defeated in the U.S. presidential election of 1984 is necessarily false because, given that it is not true in α, there is no possible world in which it is true, since there is no possible world other than α in which Reagan exists. And the proposition that Reagan is reelected in 1984 entails every true proposition (such as the proposition that there are killer whales in Puget Sound in 1980) because there is no possible world in which the former is true and the latter false, since any possible world in which the latter is false will be other than α and any possible world other than α will be a possible world in which Reagan doesn't exist and so not a possible world in which the proposition that Reagan is reelected in 1984 is true.

Nor can these unhappy consequences of rejecting cross-world identity be plausibly avoided by holding that we can "explicate" the accidental/essential distinction by appeal to the idea that things in α have "counterparts" in other possible worlds. For appeal to such a counterpart theory yields results that are as counterintuitive as Leibnizian essentialism. Suppose we adopt the view that when we say that you could have worn a different-colored tie today, what we're saying is that there is a possible world in which not you but your counterpart wears a different-colored tie on a certain day; where the object that is your counterpart in possible world *w* is the thing in *w*, if there is such a thing, that is similar to you in important respects and more similar to you in these respects than any other things in *w*.[6] Then we get the following difficulty: suppose there were a possible world *w* that contains a counterpart of me—*c*, say—and a counterpart of you—*d*, say. Then it follows, given the notion of counterparthood indicated, that there is no possible world *w'* that is qualitatively indiscernible from *w*, and in which I am indiscernible from *d* and you from *c*. But that doesn't seem right. When we think that "There but for the grace of God go I," we needn't be thinking that we could have instantiated only *some* of *x*'s purely qualitative properties.[7] And similar problems, as far as I can see, beset any conception of counterparthood.

Finally, whichever line is taken regarding cross-world identity, the advocate of the Modal Parity Thesis faces the following embarrassments as well. First, there are, on this view, an infinitude of concrete objects other than those that actually exist. Furthermore, we know this in virtue of knowing that such and such is possible. Yet how such knowledge could be acquired becomes an ineluctable mystery in view of the fact that there are no causal connections among the inhabitants of different possible worlds.[8] Second, we all hold that it is not a bad thing that horrors of all kinds are merely possible. No one thinks it appropriate to bemoan the fact that the Nazis might have won World War II, or might have developed and used nuclear weapons to destroy most of the civilized world. But if the Modal Parity Thesis is true, it would appear to be just as bad that some holocaust occurs in a nonactual possible world as that it occurs in α. Evil is evil, wherever it takes place. (It might be said, of course, that if a condition is logically necessary, then it is foolish to regret it or wish it had been otherwise. But that horrors of all kinds occur here and there in the logical space that houses the system of possible worlds is a matter of necessity and not a matter that could have been otherwise. Foolish or not, however, people do regret not being able to lead a set of incompatible lives and do wish they could spend all their energy doing physics and also all of it practicing the piano. But no one is similarly upset by the ills that might have been or could obtain but won't.) Third, the Modal Parity Thesis runs afoul of the intuition that it is a good thing, *ceteris paribus*, to prevent horrors from occurring in α. But why this should be if they occur anyway—if not in α then in another possible world—is surely puzzling, at least when the horrors to be prevented do not involve the preventer or those he especially cares about.[9] Finally, the vision of reality the Modal Parity Thesis presents is a nightmare compared to which the Augustinian/Calvinist vision seems almost benign. For the thesis entails that logical space is filled with conscious and self-conscious beings, in numbers that stagger the imagination, who undergo excruciating torture through vast (perhaps endless) stretches of time. If any views can be reasonably rejected on pragmatic grounds, this view is surely among them.

In view of considerations like the above, it would seem that there has to be a genuine distinction between the notions of truth *simpliciter* and truth-at-a world. For if there isn't, the Omega Is Special Argument goes through, with the result that the Modal Parity Thesis is correct and all the problems just detailed follow. Unfortunately, there is a budget of considerations that, taken together, provide reason for denying the distinction and so for embracing the Modal Parity Thesis. These are considerations, to which I turn next, that give support to the claim that the alternatives to denying the distinction and with it the Modal Parity Thesis are even worse. In the end, I believe such considerations are not of sufficient power to establish the claim in question. Yet for reasons that will become clear, what the best view is, all things considered, remains, in my judgment, unobvious.

Notes

1. Alvin Plantinga adopts the view that possible worlds are such collections of states of affairs. See *The Nature of Necessity* (Oxford: Oxford University Press, 1974), and "Actualism and Possible Worlds" in M. Loux, ed., *The Possible and the Actual* (Ithaca: Cornell University Press, 1979). The propositional variant has been presented by Robert M. Adams. See his "Theories of Actuality," *Nous* 8 (September 1974).

2. The argument in this paragraph is a development of the line of thought sketched in David Lewis, "Attitudes *De Dicto* and *De Se*," *Philosophical Review* 88 (October 1979): 533.

3. Cf. David Lewis, "Individuation by Acquaintance and by Stipulation," *Philosophical Review* 92 (January 1983): 21–22.

4. The line of thought in this and the preceding paragraph was suggested to me by Adams's paper "Theories of Actuality."

5. These consequences are developed in Alvin Plantinga, "Transworld Identity or Worldbound Individuals?" in M. Loux, ed., *The Possible and the Actual*.

6. This conception of counterparthood is presented by David Lewis in "Counterpart Theory and Quantified Modal Logic" in M. Loux, ed., *The Possible and the Actual,* and in *Counterfactuals* (Cambridge: Harvard University Press, 1973).

7. Cf. Fred Feldman, "Counterparts," *Journal of Philosophy* 68 (July 1, 1971).

8. This point is made by William Lycan, "The Trouble with Possible Worlds," in M. Loux, ed., *The Possible and the Actual*.

9. The last two points are made by Robert M. Adams in "Theories of Actuality."

CHAPTER FIVE

Essences, Origins, and Branching Worlds

I

In the previous chapter, I argued that thinking of nonactual possible worlds as "big, concrete particulars" that differ from the actual world not in kind but only in "what goes on at them" carries high costs. In the course of this discussion, I also indicated the main reasons for rejecting the view that entities like you and me are "world-bound," that is, of necessity confined to just one of the possible worlds, the one that happens to obtain. These considerations suggest that, unless we abjure the notion of possible worlds altogether, along with the range of modal locutions that are part and parcel of it—a course that is on the face of it no less drastic than abjuring, say, temporal or epistemic locutions—we should (a) think of possible worlds as abstract entities of some kind and (b) concede that things can exist in more than one possible world. It is not surprising that this is the course that many of those who have reflected deeply on "the metaphysics of modality" follow.

The doctrine that possible worlds are abstract entities has come to be called "Actualism" and "Moderate Modal Realism," and on one of its (prima facie) more attractive versions it takes the following form. Among the abstract entities that the world in some sense contains are entities of the sort that are expressed by phrases such as 'George Washington's having been a president of the United States', 'my being over 6' tall', and 'this desk's going to be chopped into kindling tomorrow'. Such things are commonly called "states of affairs." Some of these obtain or are actual; some do/are not. The last-mentioned state of affairs, I trust, does not obtain; the first two do. Possible worlds on the view in question are just states of affairs that are "maximal" and "possible." A state of affairs K is *maximal* just in case it is true that, for every state of affairs, S, either K includes or precludes S, where a state of affairs S* includes another S** if it is not possible that S* obtain and S** fail to obtain, and a state of affairs S* precludes another S** if it is not possible that both obtain. A state of affairs is *possible* just in case it is one that (logically) could obtain; that is, its obtaining or being actual does not entail the truth of any self-contradictory or inconsistent propositions. (A closely related conception construes possible worlds as maximal, consistent sets of propositions.) The actual world on this view is, of course, the possible world that obtains. (That only one possible world obtains follows from the fact that any two maximal states of affairs are incompossible.) Since it is a state of affairs like the other possible worlds, it too is properly thought of as an abstract entity. Moreover, this way of conceiving possible worlds readily accommodates the idea that things exist in more than one possible world. For something *a* exists in possible world *w* just in case *w* contains the state of affairs *a's existing*. Accordingly, *a* exists in both possible world *w* and possible world *w** (*w* ≠ *w**) just in case *a's existing* is a state of affairs common to both.[1]

Unfortunately, this conception of possible worlds is not problem-free either. Consider the question "If a different possible world had been actual, would I be among its denizens?" It's tempting to hold (a) that there is a correct answer to this question, either "Yes" or "No," and (b) that which of these is the correct answer depends upon what properties the individuals in the world in question possess. In particular, it is tempting to think that the answer to such a question turns on whether the features that individuate me are possessed by any "inhabitant" of the world in question. After all, something about me makes me the individual I am. But if we give up the view that it is some feature or features I possess that individuate me, we seem forced to the idea that what makes me the individual I am is merely the fact that the possessor of the properties I instantiate is what it is, quite independently of any of the features it exhibits—an idea that seems on the face of it unintelligible.

It thus appears that once we embrace a conception of possible worlds and cross-world identity of the sort discussed earlier, we are naturally led to accept the idea that each of us possesses at least one property such that nothing in any possible world that is distinct from us has it and nothing in any possible world that is identical with us lacks it. Put in a slightly different way, we find ourselves led to the view that each individual possesses at least one property P such that (a) there is no possible world in which that individual exists and lacks P, and (b) there is no possible world in which P is exemplified by something that is not strictly identical with that individual. Following a now common usage, I shall call such properties "individual essences."[2]

But this view is very problematic. For when we try to get clear about what our individual essences are, we find that none of the candidates that seem plausible is very attractive. In sections II through IV I shall explain why this is so. Then, in sections V and VI, I shall describe two possible ways out of the difficulty this discussion defines and indicate why neither of these is wholly satisfactory.

II

Consider the open sentence 'x = Leibniz'. According to some philosophers, such a sentence expresses a property, and moreover a property that is not reducible to (or analyzable into) a collection of "purely qualitative" properties[3] or indeed analyzable at all. I shall call such properties "haecceities,"[4] and the doctrine that there are such unanalyzable properties "haecceitism." It is easy to see that if haecceities in this sense exist, they will count as individual essences. For if there is such a property as being identical with Leibniz, it is surely one that Leibniz could not be without, and obviously there is no possible world in which something has it and isn't Leibniz.

However, only a little reflection is required to create the suspicion that haecceities are "creatures of darkness." To begin, it seems intuitively quite plausible to think that there are logical (or metaphysical) limits on the features beings like us might have possessed. I might have been 6'4" or red-haired, for example. Virtually no one—at least prior to reading certain tracts of philosophical literature—disputes this. But the idea that I might have been a green mothball, or a volcano, or a sneeze, or one of the prime numbers greater than 2^5, is hard to credit. On the face of it, judgments like these border on the senseless, at best. But if we accept the verdict that it is false or senseless that I might have had properties of these last kinds, we *ipso facto* embrace "essentialism," that is, the doctrine that some of our purely qualitative properties are essential to us in the sense that there is no possible world in which we exist and lack these properties. But essentialism, so defined, yields a puzzling consequence when it is combined with haecceitism, the doctrine that all individuals possess haecceities. For these two doctrines together entail that propositions like

Q (x) $(x$ exists and x = W.V.O. Quine $\supset x$ is a rational agent)

are both necessary and synthetic—given anyhow that the property of being a rational agent is one of Quine's essential properties. (If it isn't, substitute for Q the proposition

(x) $(x$ exists and x = W.V.O. Quine $\supset x$ is a non-number).)

The necessity of Q follows from the thesis that being a rational agent is one of Quine's essential properties. Its syntheticity follows from the fact that, given the sort of property a haecceity is, the property of being a rational agent is neither identical with nor a component of Quine's haecceity.

Now, synthetic necessary truths are perhaps not as such all that problematic. Propositions about the "internal structure" of tigers and the chemical constitution of water are, after all, plausibly thought to be of this kind.[5] And we have at least some understanding of how such propositions can both fail of analyticity and nonetheless hold in all possible worlds—although no doubt our understanding will have to be deepened before we feel completely comfortable with so conceiving them. But however this may be, the idea that propositions like Q might be both synthetic and necessary is another matter. There are two reasons for disquietude here. First, there is the difficulty in understanding why Quine's haecceity could not be coinstantiated with properties like being a rock, or even being a number, given the sort of property a haecceity is. After all, one might reason, if the property of being identical with Quine could not be coinstantiated with the property of being a rock, then it is hard to see why it could not also be true that anything having a certain set of purely qualitative properties cannot fail to instantiate this property, and that anything that instantiates this property cannot fail to possess the set of purely qualitative properties in question. But if the property of being identical with Quine is a haecceity, then it is difficult to see how such a purely qualitative individual essence could exist. For if Quine has a purely qualitative individual essence, why could not the property of being identical with Quine be analyzed by reference to it? In any case, there are powerful arguments against the existence of purely qualitative individual essences. (I give several of these in section IV below.)

Second, there is the difficulty in seeing how we could possibly know that there are necessary limits on the properties given haecceities can be coinstantiated with. The problem here derives, of course, from the absence of anything remotely like the sorts of causal connections that underlie and explain our knowledge of the "synthetic" truths we come to know via perception, memory, and various complex inferences from the knowledge perception and memory yield. I am reasonably confident that few will feel content with the suggestion Adams has recently made that perhaps such knowledge results from the fact that God "constructed us in such a way that we would at least commonly recognize necessary truth as necessary."[6] But he may well be right in thinking that the alternatives are even less attractive. These two difficulties are, of course, closely connected. To the extent that we find our "knowledge" of these alleged "necessary truths" puzzling, to that extent we will also feel less than confident that our haecceities couldn't be coinstantiated with such and such other properties. And independent worries on the latter issue will tend to throw in doubt the thesis that we do know that the propositions in question are indeed necessarily true.

But another line of thought also makes for skepticism as regards haecceities. It goes thus. It cannot be a necessary truth, one might think, that the only haecceities that exist are exemplified. For if that were so, since I am a contingent being my haecceity could have failed to exist. But haecceities are properties, and properties, if they exist at all, exist necessarily, that is, exist in all possible worlds.[7] Also, it seems intuitively obvious that there could have existed an individual who does not in fact exist. After all, the ovum from which I developed might not have been fertilized, and the one that would then have appeared in the following month might have been fertilized instead. And surely the individual that would have developed from that fertilized egg might not have been me or any other human being that exists or ever will exist. (Many would probably insist that he or she certainly would not have been me or any other human being that exists or ever will exist.) But what could it mean to say that an individual might have existed who does not, never did, and never will, if not that there is a possible world such that had it been actual instead of the world that is, it would have been true that some object exists that never exists in the actual world (hereafter "α")? But that, it seems, is just to say that there is a haecceity that would have been exemplified that is not

exemplified as things are. At any rate, once we have embraced haecceities, this seems a natural way of explicating the truth in question.[8]

The idea that there exist unexemplified haecceities, however, appears, upon reflection, quite unattractive. Suppose $x[x = $ Plantinga]
and $x[x = $ Plantinga*][9] are two haecceities and that the latter is never
exemplified in α. Now picture God prior to the Creation. He thinks,
"Shall I create an instance of $x[x = $ Plantinga] or an instance of $x[x = $
Plantinga*]?" He ponders. Then he decides against $x[x = $ Plantinga*]
and forms instead an intention to create an instance of $x[x = $ Plan-
tinga], an instance, furthermore, that exemplifies F, where F is a
conjunction of all the time-indexed analogues of the purely qualitative
properties that Plantinga in fact instantiates. This intention, let us
suppose, is an element of the larger intention to create the "world"
that in fact exists.[10] Before executing this grand intention, however, he
has second thoughts about whether to coinstantiate $x[x = $ Plantinga]
with F or $x[x = $ Plantinga*]. Finally, after concluding his reflections,
he says in his heart, "Let there be light, let there be an instance of $x[x
= $ Plantinga], let there be . . ." Now if there are unexemplified
haecceities, the description of the above process of deliberation and
decision, as well as the question whether God's second thoughts
involved a change of intention, make sense—or, at any rate, make
sense if we assume, perhaps falsely, that the theological story in its
general outlines makes sense. Also, the idea appears to be intelligible,
given the assumption indicated, that owing perhaps to some divine,
unconscious process—a slip of the divine tongue, so to speak—$x[x = $
Plantinga*] managed to get coinstantiated with F instead of $x[x = $
Plantinga], God's intentions to the contrary notwithstanding. But none
of these consequences is at all plausible. What, one wants to ask,
could possibly be the difference between (intending to instantiate) $x[x
= $ Plantinga] and (intending to instantiate) $x[x = $ Plantinga*], given
that each of these haecceities could be coinstantiated with exactly the
same sets of purely qualitative properties? What would the difference
consist in if the world contained an instance of $x[x = $ Plantinga*] rather
than an instance of $x[x = $ Plantinga], given that Plantinga* would
possess all of Plantinga's purely qualitative properties or anyhow the
time-indexed analogues thereof? The answer that runs "The difference
would be that the one world would contain one individual and the other
a different individual" will hardly do. For the view that things are
individuated by their haecceities is scarcely different at bottom from
the view that things are the things they are quite independently of the

properties they instantiate, a doctrine that makes individuation an impenetrable mystery.[11]

But if the thought that at least some haecceities are unexemplified is unattractive, the present line of thought continues, the doctrine that they are all exemplified is hardly more satisfactory. In the first place, this doctrine, which is sometimes called "Existentialism,"[12] appears to imply that there are no singular states of affairs involving nonactual individuals. For if there were such state of affairs, then the singular propositions that would be true if these states of affairs had obtained would also exist. And a singular proposition, it would seem, either contains the individual it is "about" or contains a constituent that "refers" to this individual. But this, it would seem, requires either that the individual in question exists or at least that unexemplified individual essences exist. But the former is impossible: clearly there do not exist any individuals that do not exist. And the latter is ruled out also if Existentialism is true. For either all individual essences are haecceities or some are not. If all are haecceities and Existentialism is true, none are unexemplified. And if there are some individual essences that are not haecceities, it is hard to see how it could be true that all haecceities are exemplified. For suppose E is such an individual essence. Then surely there will be the property of being identical with the object that would exist if E were instantiated.

But the view that there are no singular states of affairs involving nonactual individuals (and hence no singular propositions about nonactual individuals) has some highly counterintuitive consequences. Suppose we agree, for reasons of a kind indicated four paragraphs back, that there might have existed at least one individual who does not (and never has or will) exist in α. Then if there are no states of affairs involving nonactual individuals, something is possible even though there is no state of affairs (or proposition) that might have obtained (or been true) in which this possibility consists. In short, given the plausible assumption that there might have existed something that never exists in α, Existentialism entails that the possible outstrips the possibly-true, which on the face of it is scarcely intelligible.

Also, it is surely true that I am a contingent being. To concede this, however, is to hold that it is possible that I should never have existed. This, in turn, is to hold that there is a possible world in which I never exist. But if there is a possible world in which I never exist, then there is a possible world such that if it had been actual, the proposition *Robert Coburn never exists* would be true. But if there are no singular propositions about nonactual individuals, there would have been no such proposition as *Robert Coburn never exists* had the possible world in question been actual. So it seems that we are compelled by Existentialism to admit, paradoxically, that certain propositions might be true even though if they were they would not exist.[13]

One might try to avoid this result by giving up the doctrine that nothing has a property in a world unless it exists in that world. But this is a doctrine for which there appears to be a very strong argument. Suppose a has property F in world w. Then surely F is exemplified in w, and furthermore it is exemplified by something identical with a. But this is tantamount to saying that if w had been actual, a would have existed. Thus, it is very hard to deny that if something has a property in a world, it exists in that world.[14]

Still another reason for regarding Existentialism with suspicion is that it requires us to view certain possibilities as spurious that may well seem—and do seem to some—quite unexceptionable. Thus it seems quite possible that I should never have existed, and this possibility may well seem quite compatible with the world's being just as it is as regards the purely qualitative features it exhibits. If it is, then I could have failed to exist even though the world that existed instead of α was qualitatively indiscernible from α. But surely what is true of me is true of every individual. So it can appear plausible to think that there is a possible world qualitatively identical with α but containing none of the individuals α contains. But if such a possible world could exist, why could it not also be the case that there are two possible worlds, each qualitatively identical with α, but sharing no individuals with either α or each other? It is hard to see why this could not be, if the possible world in question is genuine. An Existentialist, however, is forced to deny that two such possible worlds exist. For, given that no singular propositions about nonactual individuals exist, the conceptual resources necessary to distinguish two such worlds are simply not available.[15]

The idea, then, that our individual essences might be (or include) haecceities has severe drawbacks. Unfortunately, for reasons I shall next indicate, the other candidates for our individual essences fare scarcely better.

III

Artifacts, like tables, cars, and computers, are intentionally made, usually according to some more or less determinate plan, from some preexisting hunk of matter or collection of material objects. Biological individuals, like human beings, cats, and snails, come into existence as a result of some unplanned process of development from preexisting biological entities. Probably all persisting things emerge in a way that is analogous to either intentional construction or biological development. If so, then all persisting things have an origin, where x is the *origin* of $y =_{df}$ (a) x is a set of one or more objects, severally and jointly distinct from y, from which y developed via some natural biological process or some natural process analogous to a process of biological development, or (b) x is some hunk of stuff that is distinct from y, or a collection of one or more objects that are severally and jointly distinct from y, out of which y was made intentionally and according to some plan, or from which y came to be via some nonintentional process or happenstance. In any case, most of the things in our surroundings with which we have daily commerce have origins in the sense indicated. I shall hereafter refer to an origin of the first kind as an "(a)-origin" and an origin of the second kind as a "(b)-origin."

Might the property of having such and such as its origin be an individual essence of whatever possesses this property? Or, if not a property like this, perhaps some more complex property that contains such a property as an essential constituent? It is easy to see why such a thought might be, at first blush, attractive. Could you, for example, have come into existence if the ovum from which you developed had never been fertilized? There is a strong inclination to believe that if the ovum in question had not been fertilized and the next month's egg had been fertilized instead, then you would not exist, even if the individual who developed from the fertilization of the later egg were to have been similar to you in all sorts of ways. Moreover, if we imagine a possible world in which the same sperm and egg from which you developed also exist and do unite in the way necessary to give rise via ordinary processes of development to a zygote and eventually a human being, it is equally tempting to think that that is a world in which you exist, and indeed that the human being in question is the one you are—and this even if some other human being in that world is more similar to you as you in fact are, and the individual who develops from the sperm and egg in question in that world is quite dissimilar to you as you in fact are. It is perhaps worth mentioning that there is also an argument of considerable force in support of the former intuition concerning the essentiality of (a)-origin, given the correctness of the latter intuition. Suppose that in α I develop from Jack and Jill and the essentiality of (a)-origin is false. Then there is a possible world w_1 in which I develop from two objects neither of which is identical with Jack and Jill—Hansel and Gretel, say. But if w_1 exists, surely there is also a possible world—w_2, say—in which I develop from Hansel and Gretel, and Jack and Jill also exist and give rise to an individual—c, say. But given that nothing diverse from me can have developed from Jack and Jill, it follows that in w_2 I am c. But this is impossible. So the hypothesis that a person's (a)-origin is not essential must be false.[16] (Parallel considerations can be adduced in support of the ideas that a thing's (b)-origin is essential to it and that anything in a nonactual possible world that has the same (b)-origin as an object in α cannot fail to be identical with that object.)

Despite the prima facie attractiveness of the thought that a thing's origin might enter into the construction of an individual essence of the thing, none of the obvious ways of developing this idea yields a problem-free result. First, if E, the property of having such and such as its origin, is an individual essence of an object, a, it follows from the definition of an individual essence that $(w)\,(x)\,(w$ is a possible world & x exists in w & x has E in $w \supset x = a)$. Now suppose that the property of having developed from sperm s and egg e is an individual essence of me. Then, given any world containing s and e, if a person develops from s and e in that world, that person is identical with me. But then in a possible world w in which the fertilized egg from which I developed undergoes fission in the seventh day after fertilization with the result that two distinct persons b and c develop from s and e in w, it follows that I am identical with both b and c. But that is absurd: I cannot be identical with both b and c in w, given that b and c are distinct persons.

Moreover, even the weaker doctrine of the essentiality of (a)-origin is suspect. For why could there not be a possible world in which s and e fail to exist, but nonetheless a zygote comes into existence at some point that is both qualitatively and materially identical with the zygote from which I in fact developed, at least at some stage of its existence? All that is required for this state of affairs to obtain is that such a zygote be created by God *ex nihilo,* or, if this possibility is questionable owing to doubts about the intelligibility of such creation or the idea that such a product could be materially identical with the zygote from which I developed, that such a zygote is created by superscientists who arrange to put together in the right way the very atoms and molecules that constituted the zygote from which I developed. But if such a zygote exists in w and gives rise to a human being there, this human being would seem to have as good a claim to being me as any individual in any world who develops from *s* and *e*.[17]

Parallel problems exist for the view that having such and such as its (b)-origin is an individual essence of a thing. Thus, having been made from hunk of matter *h* is obviously not a sufficient condition of being identical with this table at which I now sit—hereafter *t*—since a chair might have been made from that particular hunk and no chair in *w* is identical with *t* in α. In other words, if the wood of which *t* was made had been used to make a chair instead, then *t* would not have existed at all. Nor is a thing's (b)-origin plausibly thought—in all cases any-how—to be obviously an essential feature of it. Consider a highly complex artifact like a vacation mansion or a luxury liner. Suppose a mansion now exists and is called by its owners "Valhalla." Surely Valhalla would still exist even though the stones from which it was constructed had been quarried in Colorado rather than Montana, as long as they were qualitatively the same as the ones that were in fact used. That is, if everything else had been the same—the same kinds of materials had been used, the same architectural plan had been fol-lowed, and so forth—Valhalla would have existed, we are inclined to say, despite the fact that it had a different (b)-origin.[18]

The above considerations suggest that if the idea of a thing's origin can be used in constructing properties that have some chance of counting as individual essences of their possessors, it will have to enter into the construction in a more subtle and qualified way. One way of developing an ostensibly more adequate view—at least for artifacts—goes as follows: the property that is the individual essence of the table now before me, *t*, is not having such and such as its origin, hunk of matter *h*, say. Rather, it is (a) the property E_1 of having been made from *h*, or a hunk of matter that does not differ very much from *h* as regards its molecular constituents; in conjunction with (b) the property E_2 of being a table that was made in accordance with plan P, or a plan that does not differ very much from P; in conjunction with (c) the property E_3 of being the only P-table that could be made from *h* or an appropriate *h*-congener. At any rate, it is easy to see that property E—the complex property whose components are E_1, E_2, and E_3—might plausibly be thought to satisfy the conditions a property must satisfy to be an individual essence. Obviously E is a property that could be exemplified. And it is at least tempting to hold that it could not fail to be the case that something *x* has E iff E is essential to *x* and it is impossible that there be a *y* distinct from *x* that also has E. How, after all, could a table in some nonactual possible world be identical with a relatively simple object like *t* if it were made from some hunk of wood containing mainly different molecules from *h?* How could something in another world be *t* if it were not a table of the right sort? If *t* could lack E_3, it could contain none of the same molecules it contains in the actual world. Also, how could anything *t** in any possible world have E and yet fail to be identical with *t?* After all, *t** is a P-table made from *h* (or an appropriate *h*-congener) and the sole P-table so made. On the face of it, anything meeting these conditions must be *t.* And so on.

However, attractive as such an individual essence-candidate may at first appear, it also is not without problems. One of the central of these turns on a line of thought the main idea of which derives from Chisholm.[19] Assume that E is an individual essence of my table *t* in the sense just defined. It follows that there is a possible world w_1 in which *t* originates from a hunk of wood h_1, where h_1 differs by only one molecule from *h,* the hunk of wood which is *t*'s (b)-origin. But if w_1 exists, there must also be a possible world w_2 in which *t* originates from a hunk of wood h_2 that differs by only one molecule from h_1. And so on, until we reach a possible world w_n in which *t* originates from a hunk of wood h_n that shares no molecules at all with *h.* But if w_n exists, the assumption with which we started must be false: E cannot be an individual essence of *t* after all. So, if E is an individual essence of *t,* it is false that E is an individual essence of *t.* Hence E cannot be an individual essence of *t,* appearances to the contrary notwithstanding.

There is a way of stopping this argument. One could give up the idea that possibility is nonrelative, thus holding that the fact that w_n is possible relative to w_{n-1} and w_{n-1} possible relative to w_{n-2}, and so on, does not entail that w_n is possible relative to w_1.[20] Unfortunately, this way of avoiding the difficulty is also not without its costs. After all, if possibilities are thus relative, then certain states of affairs would be possible if reality had been different in certain ways, even though they are quite impossible as things are. Also, it would be the case that some propositions are true in all possible worlds, and hence necessary, as things are, but not true in all possible worlds, and hence contingent, had things been different in certain ways: for had things been different in certain ways, different worlds would be possible. But these ideas border on the nonsensical; at any rate, they do when they concern *metaphysical* possibility. (No one, of course, wants to deny that it would be possible for me to swim the English Channel if years ago I had undertaken a certain training program—perhaps inter alia—although as things now stand, such a feat is quite impossible for me.

Such possibilities and impossibilities concern not metaphysical, but, as we might say, "physiological" possibilities and impossibilities.) In any case, the idea of (metaphysically) impossible possible worlds and *a fortiori* the idea of (metaphysically) necessary truths that hold, so to speak, only contingently are ideas to be embraced only with great reluctance, it seems to me.

But the arguments indicated are not the only ones that bode ill for the conception of individual essences now under consideration. Yet another takes the form of a dilemma. Suppose that E is an individual essence (in the relevant sense) of this table, t. Then either there is an exact cutoff point defining how different a hunk of matter can be from the hunk from which t was in fact made, or there is a region in which there just is no fact of the matter whether a given hunk in a given possible world is sufficiently like h that the sole P-table made from it is t. But if the latter is the case, there is a collection of tables scattered around in logical space of each of which it will be true that it neither is nor is not identical with t. But that is difficult to swallow: what is the identity relation, after all, but a set of pairs of the form $\langle x,x \rangle$? Now consider the pair $\langle t,t' \rangle$, where t is our table and t' is a P-table in some nonactual possible world. Either this pair belongs to the set making up the identity relation or it doesn't. For suppose this is not so. Then $\langle t,t' \rangle$ is clearly not the same pair as $\langle t,t \rangle$. For the latter pair certainly is a member of the set defining the identity relation. But then t is distinct from t', and hence there is a fact of the matter as regards the identity of t with t'. Unfortunately, the other horn of the dilemma is equally unattractive. Surely we do not want to be forced into accepting a thesis such as that no P-table that might have existed is identical with t if it was made from a hunk of wood (h^*) which, though containing the same number of molecules as h, contained exactly 104,396 different molecules, whereas it would be t if only 104,395 of h^*'s molecules were different from h's.[21]

IV

Once we have given up the idea that there are haecceities, as well as the idea that a thing's origin might be, or play an essential role in, an individual essence of that thing, what candidates for individual essences remain? I can see only two. It might be held, first, that a thing's individual essence consists, perhaps inter alia, in some subset of its purely qualitative properties. However, the possibility that a set of purely qualitative properties that something possesses might constitute its individual essence is not really plausible. First, it is hard to rule out the existence of possible worlds that are either radially symmetrical or characterized by Nietzschean "eternal recurrence." But if this is so, it is possible that there are pairs of distinct individuals that share all their purely qualitative properties. Also, it seems clear that the sperm and egg from which you developed—let us call them 'Hansel' and 'Gretel', respectively—would have given rise to an individual with very different features had the intrauterine environment surrounding the organism resulting from their union been significantly different. And, of course, the same is true of Dick and Jane, the sperm and egg from which I developed. But if Hansel and Dick had been sufficiently similar and Gretel and Jane sufficiently similar, and the conditions surrounding the two zygotes resulting from their respective unions sufficiently different from what they in fact were, it is plausible to think that you could have had any purely qualitative properties that I possess, and conversely.

The second of the possibilities to which I have alluded is that a thing's individual essence consists of a subset of its so-called "world-indexed" properties, where a world-indexed property is the property of having some ordinary property in a certain possible world. In particular, it might be held that whenever it is the case that a possesses some property P uniquely in some possible world w, then the property of having P in w is an individual essence of a.[22]

It is easy to see why such world-indexed properties, if there are any, constitute individual essences of their possessors. Consider the property Q of having authored *The Nature of Necessity* in α. If there are such properties, then clearly something does possess Q. Moreover, it is quite plausibly thought a necessary truth that whatever has Q has it essentially (how could something be Plantinga in another possible world unless it were true of that thing that it authored *The Nature of Necessity* in α?) and also that nothing distinct from Plantinga could have it (how could a in w be distinct from Plantinga and yet have authored *The Nature of Necessity* in α?).

Unfortunately, such individuating world-indexed properties, it seems, are just haecceities in disguise, or at any rate close cousins of haecceities. They are haecceities in disguise if the logical equivalence of properties P and P* counts (or is taken as counting) as a sufficient condition of property identity, since any individuating world-indexed property is clearly logically equivalent to the corresponding haecceity, that is, the haecceity of whatever possesses the property in question. Thus, it is obviously a necessary truth that a possesses the property of being identical with Plantinga iff *a* possesses Q, since otherwise there would be a possible world containing an individual identical with Plantinga of whom it was false that he (or she) authored *The Nature of Necessity* in α. They are, on the other hand, at least close cousins of haecceities if a more fine-grained criterion of property identity is accepted/adopted. For like haecceities, they are, if they exist, individual essences of the things that possess them and individual essences that are neither reducible to purely qualitative properties, nor such as to involve the idea of origin. (If they were so reducible, there would be individual essences that are made up of purely qualitative properties or individual essences that essentially involve the notion of origin.) In either case, they inherit the problems we have seen to beset haecceities.

This is obvious, of course, if they just are haecceities. But it appears to be true even if they are only close cousins of haecceities. For consider. Either all such world-indexed properties are actually exemplified, or some are not. Suppose the former. Then, as before, there will be no singular propositions about nonexistent individuals, and all the counterintuitive consequences that fact was shown to entail will be unavoidable. On the other hand, if some individuating world-indexed properties are unexemplified, we again have to swallow the idea that there are properties just as empty as haecceities appear to be. In other words, unexemplified, individuating world-indexed properties serve just as well as haecceities in the Creation-story described earlier. (Instead of $x[x = $ Plantinga] and $x[x = $ Plantinga*], substitute $x[x$ authors *The Nature of Necessity* in w] and $x[x$ authors *The Nature of Necessity* in w'], understanding the former to be exemplified in α and the latter not.) So their (ostensible) unintelligibility seems to count as well against the idea that there are unexemplified, individuating world-indexed properties. Indeed, one might wonder how an actually unexemplified property like $x[x$ and x alone has P in w]—Z, say—could exist without its also being true that there is a corresponding haecceity H. After all, Z is an individual essence of whatever has it. So if Z exists, how could there fail to be the haecceity of the individual whose individual essence Z would be were w to be actual?

V

So far I have set out a line of thought that leads to the conclusion that each of us possesses an individual essence, and I have shown that each of the prima facie possible views about what sorts of properties our alleged individual essences might be carries highly counterintuitive consequences. I turn in this and the following section to a consideration of some ways in which it might be thought that we could sidestep the problem that gives rise to these difficulties and give reasons for thinking that neither is very satisfactory.

The question that led to the apparent need for individual essences, it will be recalled, was this: If a different possible world, *w,* had been actual, would I be among *w*'s inhabitants? The suggestion was that there must be an answer to this question and that this answer will depend upon whether among the denizens of *w* there is one that has my individuating feature(s)—my individual essence. But, it might be said, there is a different and more appropriate response that does not saddle us with individual essences. It goes thus. Would I exist if *w* were actual? That depends upon *w*'s correct description. If the correct description of *w* includes a sentence containing a rigid designator of me—my name, for example—then I am in *w*. If it contains no such designator, there are two possibilities. Either I am not there or there just is no answer to the question whether I am there. The former will be the case if the correct description of *w* is such that every individual in *w* is referred to by a rigid designator that, of course, refers as well to an individual in α. In that case *w* is a world that contains a proper subset of α's individuals (and none besides), and I am among the individuals that α contains that *w* lacks. It will also be the case if all of the individuals in *w* that are not referred to by rigid designators lack my essential properties, assuming I have some such properties. The latter will be the case if there are (at least) some individuals in *w* that possess whatever essential properties I possess and are designated in the description of *w* by means of referring devices that are not rigid designators. The reason there will in this case be no answer to the question whether I am in *w* is not that the concept of identity is vague. (That is an idea we do well to scotch for reasons mentioned in section III above.) It's rather that in this case the description of *w* is incomplete. In other words, the question whether I am in *w* has no answer— there just is no fact of the matter as to whether I am there or not— because the description is such that a number of distinct worlds all satisfy it, in some of which I am present and in others of which I am not.[23]

Does this sort of response to the question under consideration obviate the need for individual essences? Not if a realistic attitude toward possible worlds is reasonable; that is, not if it is plausible to think of possible worlds as proper objects for the quantifiers in our canonically expressed theory of reality to range over. For then nonactual possible worlds are, in Russell's memorable phrase, "part of the furniture of the world." And if this is so, it surely is intelligible to ask in virtue of what the correct description of one of these worlds, *w,* contains the sentence S ('Alvin Plantinga authors *The Nature of Necessity*') rather than S* ('Robert M. Adams authors *The Nature of Necessity*'). But if such a question makes sense, surely the answer will have to be that the individual who authors *The Nature of Necessity* in *w* has (or lacks) the property (or properties) that (singly or together) Plantinga cannot lack and that nothing distinct from Plantinga can possess. After all, if the object in *w* who authors *The Nature of Necessity—a,* say—lacks any individuating property of Plantinga, it clearly is not correctly designated by the rigid designator 'Alvin Plantinga', and if *a* has Plantinga's individuating property (or properties), it cannot fail to be Plantinga.

Also, it is worth noting that even if one could see how to avoid commitment to individual essences via the way of thinking about cross-world identity that involves appeal to descriptions of possible worlds that employ rigid designators, one would still face some of the same problems that beset proponents of individual essences. For suppose there are no individual essences in the sense given this expression in section I, and also suppose that it makes sense to identify individuals across possible worlds only when these worlds are characterized by the use of rigid designators that designate actual individuals. (Without individual essences that can be grasped independently of acquaintance with [or knowledge of] their actual instances, it is hard to see how there could be rigid designators of nonactual individuals.) Then, it would seem, there will be no singular propositions about nonactual individuals. For no such propositions will be within our intellectual grasp—and this as a matter of metaphysical necessity—and the idea that there might be propositions that we are *of metaphysical necessity* precluded from grasping is hard to accept.[24] But if there are no singular propositions about nonactual individuals, once again we find ourselves having to affirm, counterintuitively, that the possible is not exhausted by the possibly-true, since there will be worlds that could have been actual which have the feature that if they had been actual, propositions would be true that do not, as things stand, even exist.

VI

A quite different way of avoiding the problems developed in sections II through IV above involves appeal to the idea of "branching worlds."

The central thought here would be that by thinking about possible worlds in a different way we can both retain a realistic attitude toward them and also allow for cross-world identity while avoiding commitment to any individual essences of a questionable sort. The different way of thinking about (nonactual) possible worlds involves viewing each, as before, as a maximal, possible state of affairs but, in addition, as a state of affairs that (so to speak) branches off the actual world now or at some time earlier than the present, and thus as being identical with the actual world throughout at least part of its history, viz., the part prior to the point of branching. In other words, each nonactual possible world is a possible but unrealized future outcome of either the present state of affairs or some past state of affairs, together with the entire past of that present or past state of affairs.[25] Moreover, on this way of conceiving modal matters, an object b in a nonactual possible world w is identical with some object a that exists in the actual world iff b comes into existence in w at some point prior to the point of branching—t, say—and $b = a$ prior to t. Thus, there is a possible world in which I am a lawyer only if there is a possible world that branches off from α after I come into existence and which contains a lawyer who is related in the right way to me as I was before the time of branching.[26] And if I am essentially not a rock, that is, a non-rock in all the possible worlds in which I exist, then for each nonactual possible world w it is true either that I am not among its inhabitants— which will be true if w branches from α before I come into existence— or (a) none of the rocks that exist in the part of w that α shares is identical with me and (b) none of the rocks that exist in that part of w that diverges from α is crosstemporally identical with an object that exists prior to the fork and which is identical with me.[27] Accordingly, if the question is raised whether if some nonactual possible world w had been actual I would be there, the answer can be given without recourse to the idea of individual essences. The answer will be "Yes" iff w branches off α at some point after I come into existence in α; and the answer will be "No" otherwise, that is, "No," provided w branches off α at some point before I come into existence in α.

The branching conception, as I shall call the conception just described, is attractive not just because it avoids the need for individual essences. It also appeals to some because it rules out as spurious certain "possible" worlds that adherents of other conceptions seem forced to embrace. Consider, for example, the "possible" world w in which Napoleon and I "trade places," though w and α are qualitatively indiscernible. On conceptions like the one described in the earlier part of this chapter, it is hard to see why w is not a genuine world, assuming that all of my essential properties are shared by Napoleon, and conversely.[28] But many feel it is more plausible to deny that w is genuine and to explain the inclination to think otherwise as resulting from our capacity to imagine having various of Napoleon's features and occupying his role in history, than it is to accept the idea that, yes, things could have been just as they are qualitatively, even though it was I who invaded Russia and fought unsuccessfully at Waterloo and Napoleon who reflected on the metaphysics of modality in the 1980s.[29] And this is exactly the result that the branching conception yields, since there is no way on that conception for it to be genuinely possible that I and Napoleon should trade features and role. For one thing, any world in which another had Napoleon's features and role would have had to branch off from α before I came into existence, and hence would lack me.

In addition, the branching conception provides a way of sidestepping the dilemma that arises once one supposes, as it seems natural to do once one embraces the earlier conception, that a table t could have been made from a hunk of wood that differed by a molecule or two from the hunk of wood from which it was in fact made. I allude here to the difficulties that arise from holding either that there is an exact cutoff point defining how different a hunk of matter can be from the hunk h from which t was in fact made, or that there is a region in which there just is no fact of the matter whether a given hunk of wood in a given possible world is sufficiently like h as regards its molecular constituents that the sole table made from it, in accordance with plan P, is or is not (identical with) t. (The difficulties in question are presented in the last paragraph of section III.) This is so because on this conception a table (t^*) in some nonactual world (w) is identical with t, the table at which I now sit, only provided w branches off from α after t comes into existence and t^* is identical with t prior to the fork. Thus, according to the branching conception, t simply could not have originated from some hunk of matter in any way different from the hunk of matter from which it did in fact originate.

Last, the branching conception is attractive because it entails the falsity of the doctrine that the property of having originated from such and such objects or material is a sufficient condition of cross-world identity, which is just as it should be. For suppose I in fact developed from sperm s and egg e and so did b in possible world w that is distinct from α. It does not follow on the branching conception that b and I are identical. For w might have branched off from α before I came into existence, assuming that I am not strictly identical with any zygote that existed in the past; and if it did, then, on the branching view, I do not exist in w.

Unfortunately, this conception of possible worlds and cross-world identity also abounds in paradox. No one, I am sure, thinks it would be correct to say of a bushel of acorns that the bushel contains 279 oak trees. It is similarly incorrect, it seems to me, to include the zygotes when one gives the number of persons currently living in New York City. (Which is not, of course, to deny that a zygote in a woman's womb is either human or a living organism. But to infer from the fact that such zygotes are living human organisms the proposition that they are human beings [or persons] would be legitimate only if it were also legitimate to infer that the sperm produced in human testes are human beings [or persons]. After all, they too are human and living organisms.) But if a zygote is not a human being (or person), then I am identical with a certain zygote that existed in the past only if I am not essentially a human being or something that has experiences or something that possesses a body with at least a rudimentary nervous system. But if it is true that I am distinct from the zygote from which I developed, then on the branching conception there is no possible world in which I am, say, blind owing to damage to that zygote seven days after fertilization of the ovum from which it developed. For any possible world in which some person develops from such a damaged zygote *ex hypothesi* branches from α prior to my coming into existence, and hence is a world from which I am absent. But surely we want to hold that I could have been blind owing to some unfortunate occurrence inside my mother prior to my having emerged in the course of fetal development.[30]

Again, consider the question whether Franklin Delano Roosevelt, who in fact died in 1945, could have seen my sister, who was born in 1947. Intuitively, it seems to me, we want to say that this is possible. After all, FDR could have lived a few years longer, that is, it is at least logically possible that he should have. And if he had, it is at least logically possible that he should have seen my sister shortly after her birth. At any rate, it is easy to tell a coherent story in which such things take place. But on the branching conception, such a thing happening is impossible, because on that conception any possible world in which FDR's life ends later than 1945 is a world that branches off α prior to 1947, and any world that branches off α prior to 1947 is a world that lacks my sister. For similar reasons it is not possible on the branching conception for my sister ever to have seen FDR, except in photos or old news reels. For any nonactual possible world in which my sister exists is just like α up to 1947 and hence is a world in which FDR dies in 1945.

Indeed, the situation is even worse than the above considerations bring out. Since on the branching conception my brother does not exist in any nonactual possible world that is not exactly like α up to the time at which he comes into existence, it follows that if he came into existence in a room with purple wallpaper, he has as an essential property that he came into existence in a room with purple wallpaper. And if his wife's father wore purple socks on his third birthday, it is an essential property of my brother's that his father-in-law wore purple socks on his third birthday. In short, the branching conception has the unpalatable consequence that any property my brother had when he first came into existence—not excluding relational properties of the sort just mentioned—is a property that he has in any world in which he exists and so is, on the standard view, an essential property of his.[31]

Finally, the branching conception entails that what is possible at one time is different from what is possible at an earlier or later time; in other words, that the possible is temporally relative. This is so because, on this way of developing the metaphysics of modality, after Napoleon, for example, comes into existence there are nonactual possible worlds containing Napoleon, whereas before he came into existence there simply were no such worlds. For suppose there were such worlds. Then there would be worlds containing Napoleon that branch off α before Napoleon comes into existence. After all, there would be all sorts of states of affairs involving Napoleon, and what could prevent their being assembled with others to make up world-size states of affairs that involve Napoleon living in the 15th century A.D.? Thus, if we combine the idea that possible worlds are maximal, possible states of affairs with the requirements on cross-world identity that are also built into the branching conception, there is no alternative to holding that what states of affairs (and so possible worlds) exist is temporally relative. But this consequence runs counter to firm intuitions at a number of points.[32]

Suppose one of the nonactual possible worlds that branches off from α before I came into existence had been actual. Then not only would it be the case that I never exist, but it would also be true that α is not, and never will be, among the possible worlds that exist. For if α did (or will) exist, even if one of the nonactual possible worlds that branches off from α earlier than my emergence had been actual, it is false that I am a member of only those nonactual possible worlds that branch from the actual world after I come into existence. For if α did (or will) exist, in the case imagined, there is (or will be) a nonactual possible world such that (a) if it had been actual I would exist and such that (b) it does not branch off from the world that is actual at some time later than the time of my emergence onto the scene. Suppose w is a nonactual possible world that branches from α at t_1 and that I in fact came into existence at t_2. This situation is depicted in Figure 5.1.

Figure 5.1

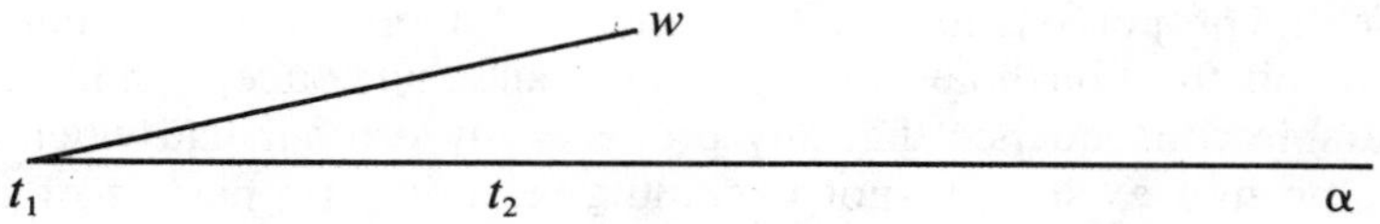

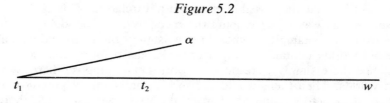

Now suppose that w had been actual and that α was among the nonactual possible worlds. This situation is depicted in Figure 5.2.

Figure 5.2

Then it would be the case that a nonactual possible world, viz. α, would exist containing me, even though it branches off from the world that is actual, viz. w, before t_2. But the idea that the actual world would not have been among the possible worlds (that ever exist) had things turned out differently is hard to swallow. Surely if anything is clear in this area of metaphysics, it is clear that if something does happen, it could happen; that what happens today was at least possible yesterday.[33] And equally difficult to accept is the thought that the proposition *Robert Coburn never exists* might have been true, even though if it had been, there would have been no such proposition.[34]

Also, the idea that possible worlds—worlds, for example, in which Napoleon dies of cancer at age 21—come into existence once, say, Napoleon appears that did not exist *in any sense* prior to a certain date, is tantamount to the idea that there is a nonrelative distinction between past, present, and future (that it is false that every event, for example, is past, since what it is to be past is just to be earlier than certain later events or times) and that what is commonsensically spoken of as "the passage of time" involves irreducible, objective (mind-independent) changes as, for example, Christmas 1994 and Easter 1998 draw steadily closer to the present with each passing day.[35] But as I shall make clear in the next chapter, this view about what temporal passage involves entails the existence of facts—such as that today is November 20, 1988—that are both irreducible and ineluctably "fugitive," that is, facts into the expression of which temporal indexicals enter essentially, and there are powerful reasons for doubting that any facts of this kind are part of the warp and woof of existence.

It appears, then, that an appeal to the branching conception of possible worlds and cross-world identity will not help us toward a problem-free escape from the difficulties canvassed earlier.

VII

What are we to conclude from this recital of apparently intractable problems? We should conclude, first, that here as elsewhere the most acceptable view will, in all probability, fall short of meeting all the desiderata that we might wish it to meet. But a second conclusion also strikes me as reasonable, namely, that further work may have to be done in this area of metaphysics before we even glimpse the contours of what will eventually appear to be a reasonably attractive view.

Notes

1. This conception of possible worlds is due to Alvin Plantinga. See especially *The Nature of Necessity* (Oxford: Oxford University Press, 1974), and "Actualism and Possible Worlds" in M. Loux, ed., *The Possible and the Actual* (Ithaca: Cornell University Press, 1979).

2. See, for example, A. Plantinga, "De Essentia," in E. Sosa, ed., *Essays on the Philosophy of Roderick M. Chisholm* (Amsterdam: Rodopi, 1979).

3. One way of explicating this notion is given by R. M. Adams thus: P is a purely qualitative property just in case "it could be expressed, in a language sufficiently rich, without the aid of such referential devices as proper names, proper adjectives and verbs (such as 'Leibnizean' and 'pegasizes'), indexical expressions, and referential uses of definite descriptions." See his "Primitive Thisness and Primitive Identity," *Journal of Philosophy* 76 (1979): 17.

4. Haecceities in my sense are referred to by R. M. Adams as "primitive thisnesses." See his papers "Primitive Thisness and Primitive Identity" and

"Actualism and Thisness," *Synthese* 49 (1981). (N.B.: Adams uses 'haecceity' and 'thisness' to express the same concept.)

5. See Saul Kripke, *Naming and Necessity* (Cambridge: Harvard University Press, 1972), Lecture III.

6. R. M. Adams, "Divine Necessity," *Journal of Philosophy* 80 (1983): 751.

7. This line of thought is suggested by A. Plantinga, "Actualism and Possible Worlds," p. 262.

8. Plantinga suggests this way of understanding the truth in question in ibid., pp. 268 ff.

9. I occasionally use Quine's method for forming names of properties and relations. See *Word and Object* (New York: John Wiley, 1960), p. 164 f.

10. I put 'world' in quotes to underscore the fact that the created world is not identical with α if God exists, since he is then also an inhabitant of α.

11. The basic line of thought in this paragraph is an adaptation of an argument in A. N. Prior, "Identifiable Individuals," in *Papers on Time and Tense* (Oxford: Clarendon Press, 1968), p. 718.

12. This use of the word is Plantinga's. See "On Existentialism," *Philosophical Studies* 44 (1983).

13. This consequence of Existentialism is brought out in R. M. Adams, "Actualism and Thisness," especially in sec. 3.

14. The thesis that nothing has a property in a world unless it exists in that world is sometimes called "serious actualism." The argument indicated for this thesis is given by A. Plantinga in his "Reply to Pollock," in James Tomberlin and Peter van Inwagen, eds., *Alvin Plantinga: A Profile* (Dordrecht: D. Reidel, 1984).

15. This implication of Existentialism is also discussed by Adams in "Actualism and Thisness," sec. 4.3.

16. The basic structure of this line of thought derives from Kripke, *Naming and Necessity,* p. 114 f., n. 56.

17. This counterexample appears in M. Price, "On the Non-Necessity of Origin," *Canadian Journal of Philosophy* 12 (1982).

18. Cf. P. F. Strawson, "May Bes and Might Have Beens," in A. Margalit, ed., *Meaning and Use* (Dordrecht: D. Reidel, 1979).

19. See R. M. Chisholm, "Identity Across Possible Worlds: Some Questions," in M. Loux, ed., *The Possible and the Actual.*

20. This is Salmon's way of dealing with such an argument. See *Reference and Essence* (Princeton: Princeton University Press, 1981), sec. 28.

21. This last line of thought was suggested to me by the line Nathan Salmon takes in his paper "Modal Paradox: Parts and Counterparts, Points and Counterpoints," in P. French, T. Uehling, Jr., and H. Wettstein, eds., *Midwest Studies in Philosophy,* Vol. 11 ("Studies in Existentialism") (Minneapolis: University of Minnesota Press, 1986). The argument against the vagueness of identity is more fully developed in ibid. (Appendix) and in *Reference and Essence,* pp. 243 ff.

CHAPTER SIX

The Passage of Time

I

Another idea that pervades everyday thought and speech is the idea of time, together with such cognate notions as objects changing, coming into existence, ceasing to exist; events and times being future, present, and past; sentences and beliefs becoming true and ceasing to be true; and so on. And these ideas also, upon reflection, cause great perplexity. In this chapter I shall seek to substantiate this claim by focusing on just one central and extremely tempting thesis involving this cluster of ideas, a thesis I shall call "the doctrine of the objectivity of temporal passage" or more briefly "the doctrine of passage."

Before I indicate what this doctrine asserts, a few preliminary matters need to be laid out. Consider any arbitrary stretch (or interval) of time—the time it takes for the earth to make one complete revolution, for example, or the time it takes for a photon to travel one centimeter. Then the whole of time can be conceived—relative to a frame of reference[1]—as a series of nonoverlapping intervals of this length, a series that has neither beginning nor end and each member of which is related to its successors by the transitive, asymmetrical, irreflexive relation *earlier than,* and to its predecessors by the converse relation *later than.* Moreover, each interval making up this doubly open series can in turn be viewed as consisting of a finite series of nonoverlapping intervals with the same structure, and so on ad indefinitum.

Following a terminological convention first introduced by Mc-Taggart,[2] I shall call such an infinite series a B-series, and corresponding to each B-series so constructed is what—again following Mc-Taggart—I will call an A-series. It consists of the same set of intervals arranged in the same order; however, here the order is determined by the A-characteristics of the individual intervals, where A-characteristics are features such as being present, being such and such a temporal distance in the future, and being such and such a temporal distance in the past, temporal distances being defined by the number of intervals separating the interval in question from the one that is present.[3] Thus, if interval k is fifteen units in the future, it is a successor of interval j, which is only fourteen units in the future, and a predecessor of m, which is seventeen units in the future, and so on.

With these remarks by way of background, the doctrine of passage asserts that it is a matter of objective (that is, mind-independent) fact that the A-characteristics of the (nonoverlapping) intervals making up any A-series are continually changing, and in a systematic way. Take, for example, the stretch of time—s, say—that is now fifteen units later than the present, on some choice of interval and unit of temporal distance. After the interval that is now taking place has elapsed and its immediate successor has become present, s will take on the A-characteristic of being only fourteen units from the present. Also, a stretch that was 1800 units in the past will then be 1801 units in the past, and so on. Further, these "changes" are objective (mind-independent) in the sense that they would occur just as they do even if there were no conscious beings in existence, never had been, and never will be. Since events that will happen but haven't yet happened, objects that once existed but no longer exist, processes that are now taking place, and so forth, can also be spoken of as possessing properties such as beginning to exist during the interval with such and such an A-characteristic, occurring at intervals with such and such A-characteristics, and so forth, the doctrine *a fortiori* asserts that "occupants" of time—events, objects, processes, etc.—also are objectively undergoing continual changes in virtue of the continual changes in the A-characteristics of the temporal stretches that they occupy in whole or part.

II

On the face of it, the doctrine of passage is quite attractive; indeed it may initially appear impossible to doubt. In any case, a variety of considerations can be adduced in its support.

The first of these is just that we both understand and know to be true (utterances of) sentences like 'The day of my flight to Dallas is approaching', 'My root canal treatment will soon be over', and 'The era of the Vietnam war is slipping further into the past all the time'. But if this is so, there must be facts that make such utterances true in the same way that the fact that my cat was fixed in 1978 makes an utterance of the sentence 'My cat was fixed in 1978' true. But what could these facts be but facts of just the sort the doctrine of passage asserts to hold, namely, facts such as that a certain stretch of time is changing its A-characteristics in the way the doctrine asserts, that a certain event occupies an interval that is similarly changing its A-characteristics, and the like?

In addition, it is widely recognized that there is a deep difference between the past and the future, a difference that is commonly expressed by talk of the latter's being "open" or "indeterminate" and the former's being "settled" or "fixed." What considerations are needed to elucidate fully what this difference amounts to may not be clear. But intuitively the difference appears to involve at least the following matters. First, we feel that nothing can be done to alter the past. We can do nothing now about the outcome of the U.S. presidential election of 1980. We might have been able to bring about a different outcome if we'd done such and such in 1979, but now it's too late. On the other hand, the outcome of the U.S. presidential election of 1992 is "undecided." It could go either way, or perhaps not occur at all. Moreover, which way it goes—assuming it will occur—may well be, we are inclined to think, up to us. At any rate, we can do things now and in the immediate future—so we believe—that may well determine (or help determine) which way the election goes. Second, facts about the past, we are inclined to believe, are "knowable in principle," at least in vast numbers of cases; that is, it is "possible in principle" that someone now or in the future should know that such facts obtain. They are "there to be known," so to speak. The outcome of the U.S. presidential election of 1992, on the other hand, is not "there to be known." For this reason it is not even in principle possible that someone should know now what it will be. Third, there is a connection between the features of the past and the future just indicated. Because the past is "there to be known," we cannot now affect it, and because the future is not "there to be known," exactly what form it will take is, we feel, up to us, at least within certain limits.

But now this difference between the past and the future appears to require a continuous objective process of the sort the doctrine of passage asserts. For in the absence of such a process, how could the one realm come to possess the features of the other? How could the blank canvas of the future be transformed into the completed painting of the past? In brief, then, the falsity of the doctrine of passage appears to be incompatible with the view that while the past is fixed the future is open, a view we are also loathe to relinquish.

Closely connected with this last line of thought is the following argument that links the doctrine of passage to the widely held conviction that we frequently have it within our power both to do and to refrain from doing various things and in consequence are frequently justly praised or blamed for doing what we do. Suppose, this argument begins, that the doctrine of passage is false. Then the distinction between the past and the future will be "relative." That is, a given occurrence—the U.S. presidential election of 1980, say—will be past relative to times later than 1980 and future relative to dates earlier than 1980; but there will be no nonrelative sense in which this event is past. But this means that all of the "contents" of time—past, present and future—have exactly the same status. In particular, the U.S. presidential election of 1992 is no less real (or "there to be known") than the U.S. presidential election of 1960, since it too is past in exactly the same sense in which the U.S. presidential election of 1960 is past. But, the argument then continues, if this is so, then the future is not open or indeterminate in any way which does not hold of the past as well. And this, in turn, means that, in a certain sense, no one can do anything other than just what he does do.

To clarify the sense in which this last thesis is true, suppose, perhaps *per impossibile,* that backward time travel is possible, and that I decide to go back to 1963 in order to assassinate John Kennedy 15 minutes before he was in fact shot. Suppose I have made the journey, and on the morning of November 22, 1963, I am well-situated to do the job and have my gun in readiness. Since I didn't shoot Kennedy as a matter of fact, I clearly won't be able to carry out my intention— assuming anyhow (as we all do) that the past can't be changed. I can perform only those actions that I did in fact perform. But now what is true of the past is also true of the future if the doctrine of passage is false. I can perform only those actions that I will in fact perform. To be sure, it is true that I can shoot Kennedy in the sense that there is a possible world just like (or close to) the actual world up to the time in question and in which I do shoot him. And in the same sense I can fly to Denver tomorrow, even though I don't. Nonetheless, if the doctrine of passage is false, it seems that there is a sense in which we cannot do anything other than what we do do—viz., the sense in which I can't shoot Kennedy 15 minutes before he was in fact shot—and this implication seems to go against the firm conviction we have concerning our power to determine what will happen in the future.[4]

Yet another line of thought that makes the doctrine of passage attractive appeals to an apparent connection between the reality of passage and the fact of change. Suppose that what change involves is simply something's having a property at one time that it lacks at another, such as a person weighing 170 lbs. on her thirtieth birthday and 135 lbs. on her seventy-fourth birthday. If the doctrine of passage is false, the future will, as just noted, be as fixed and determinate as the past. But if this is so, then to say that a has property P at t and property P* at $t'(t<t')$—where 'P*' designates the complement of P, that is, the property of not having P—is no different from saying that a has the property of having P at t (call it 'P-at-t') and the property of having P* at t' (call it 'P*-at-t''). But these latter properties are obviously properties a has "omnitemporally," that is, at every moment during which it exists. But if this is right, it's hard to see that the world can contain any genuine changes at all. Since nothing ever gains or loses any of its time-indexed properties, and every fact to the effect that something has a property at a time is reducible to a fact concerning its possession of such a time-indexed property, nothing ever really changes. But the reality of change is an undeniable fact of experience. Hence passage must be real.

Then, too, there is the following argument for the doctrine of passage. Suppose the doctrine is true. Then there will be facts—such as that today is April 20, 1985—the holding of which is a temporary matter, and there will be propositions that these facts make true, propositions that accordingly will change their truth-values with the passage of time. (Such facts are sometimes called "tensed facts"[5] and such propositions "fugitive propositions"[6]; hereafter, I shall also speak of them respectively as "A-facts" and "A-propositions.") Indeed, the doctrine of passage can be viewed as simply asserting the (irreducible) existence of facts and propositions of these kinds—at any rate, assuming (as seems plausible) that if such facts and propositions exist and are not reducible to facts and propositions of some quite distinct kind, their existence is an objective (mind-independent) matter. It follows that if the doctrine of passage is false, the fact I state when I say, for instance, that today is April 20, 1985, is not a "tensed fact," and the proposition I express is not a "fugitive proposition." But this in turn implies (a) that what makes what I say in this case true is a timeless state of affairs (one that holds at every time) and (b) that the proposition I express in saying what I say is "eternal" (always true if ever true and always false if ever false). If, however, (a) and (b) are the case, how could it fail to be true that any sentence that expresses this timeless state of affairs or the eternal proposition in question is equivalent in meaning to what I say when I say that today is April 20, 1985? But it seems upon reflection clearly false that there is any sentence that expresses a timeless state of affairs or an eternal proposition and that also has the same meaning as does my remark that today is April 20, 1985. Consider, for example, the sentence 'April 20, 1985, is April 20, 1985'. It clearly expresses a timeless state of affairs and an eternal proposition. But it certainly doesn't have the same meaning as my remark that today is April 20, 1985, for that remark might well be false. But the sentence in question can't be false. Nor will the following sentence do: 'The day that is simultaneous with my remark that today is April 20, 1985, is April 20, 1985'. For although it also clearly expresses a timeless state of affairs and an eternal proposition, no one would be inclined to hold that it has the same meaning as my remark that today is April 20, 1985. For one thing, it involves in an essential way the notion of simultaneity, whereas my remark does not. Also, the meaning of 'today' is not identical with the meaning of 'the day that is simultaneous with my remark that today is April 20, 1985'. For if yesterday someone said 'Today is April 19, 1985', she wouldn't be saying that the day that is simultaneous with my remark that today is April 20, 1985, is April 19, 1985.

Still another consideration in support of the doctrine of passage turns on certain intuitions about propositional identity. Consider a descendant of Rip Van Winkle, Rip*, who dozes off from 1900 to 1950. And suppose that right before slipping off, the thought occurs to Rip* that it's now 1900 and that when he awakens half a century later that very thought is still in his mind, that is, as soon as consciousness returns, he thinks "It's now 1900." It's certainly plausible to suppose that the proposition he entertained and judged to be true upon falling asleep is identical with the proposition he entertained and judged to be true upon awakening. After all, he'd use the same form of words to express his thought on both occasions. He might insist, once aware that he'd fallen off, that he'd not changed his mind and that he believed upon awakening exactly what he believed when he dozed off. We can well imagine that any nonverbal evidence an onlooker might have had (or gotten) in 1900 that Rip* believed then that it was 1900, an observer of Rip* when he awoke in 1950 might also have had (or gotten). Indeed, we could even build into the case that the state of Rip*'s brain at the moment he became unconscious in 1900 was qualitatively indiscernible from the state of his brain upon awakening in 1950—implausible as this might be regarding an actual case of a 50-year doze or coma. But now, this line of argument concludes, if the proposition Rip* believed at the moment he lost consciousness in 1900 is the very same proposition he believed upon awakening in 1950, then there are fugitive propositions. For the proposition he believed in 1900 is true and the proposition he believed upon awakening in 1950 is false. But fugitive propositions, if they exist, are made true (and false) by tensed facts. Such facts, in other words, constitute the truth-conditions of propositions of this kind. And it is the reality of tensed facts (and fugitive propositions) that the doctrine of passage asserts.

Last is the line of argument that appeals to the fact that when we say something like "I'm glad that my laminectomy is in the past," we appear to be expressing gladness that the event in question has a certain A-characteristic, viz., the characteristic of being earlier than the present. We're certainly not expressing gladness that the event's date is earlier than the date of the day that is now present. For that could be expressed before the laminectomy took place! But if this is right, then we sometimes have attitudes towards A-facts, attitudes that can't even be expressed without assuming the existence of such facts. But the existence of such facts, as has been repeatedly noted, is tantamount to the truth of the doctrine of passage.[7] A similar line of thought can be developed in connection with judgments like "I wish that it were now 1930." When we make this kind of statement we're not expressing a wish that a certain date bore a timeless (unchanging) relation to some other date—that 1930 were identical with 1985. Rather, we're expressing a wish that a certain date had a certain A-characteristic that it once had but no longer has.[8]

III

Despite the prima facie force of considerations like the foregoing, there appear to be strong reasons to doubt the truth of the doctrine of passage.

Consider, first, the following line of argument. If the doctrine of passage were true, then the actual world is a world in which stretches of time undergo objective changes in their A-characteristics, and the "occupants" of these stretches undergo changes in such A-characteristic-related features as "beginning to exist during an interval that has such and such an A-characteristic." But if this is so, it is difficult to see why the world couldn't have been just as it is except that the A-changes that actually take place take place more slowly or more quickly, or even in a different direction. In other words, if the doctrine of passage is true, it appears that it could have been true that the world was exactly as it is except that future events, for example, move toward the present more slowly or more quickly than they do as things are, and even that stretches of time that are later than the present stretch become increasingly further from the present and stretches of time that are earlier than the present stretch become increasingly close to the present and eventually become present and then future. Also, it's difficult to see why the world couldn't have been just as it is except that there simply are no A-changes, that is, no changes of the sort the doctrine of passage asserts. It does not, after all, seem to be a necessary truth that if a world has a temporal aspect, contains things or events that exist or happen in time, that the A-characteristics of intervals of time change in just the ways they (ostensibly) do, at just that rate and in just that direction, or indeed that they change at all.

But, the argument continues, it's false that these possibilities obtain; it is false that the world could have satisfied any of the descriptions just indicated. To begin, suppose that there were a possible world that could have been actual in place of the world that is actual, and that is exactly like the actual world except that its A-changes take place at a different rate. Then there would have to exist some periodic process by reference to which sense could be made of the notion that alleged A-changes in the one occur at a different rate than the A-changes in the other. But such a "clock" could not exist in either world. For if it did, it could not be used to measure the A-changes in either. How, for example, could a periodic process that exists in some merely possible world function to measure A-changes in the actual world? It would have to make sense to say that the secondhand of a clock in *b* is now at 12. But that would make sense only if the event in *b* were part of the temporal system of *a*, which *ex hypothesi* it is not. Nor, for similar reasons, could it exist in some third possible world and still serve the desired purpose. So it would have to exist, as it were, outside the system of possible worlds: it would have to be "God's wristwatch" (see Figure 6.1). But since everything that could exist but doesn't exists in some nonactual possible world and everything that does exist exists in the possible world that is actual, the idea of such a clock that exists outside the system of possible worlds makes no sense either.

The situation is no better concerning the other putative possibilities—the possible world, that is, in which A-changes go in the opposite

Figure 6.1

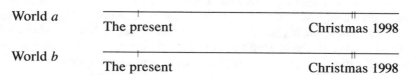

Possible world *b* is just like the actual world *a* except that in *b* Christmas 1998 covers the ten year period separating it from the present in 12 "minutes" of supertime, whereas in *a* it takes 98 "minutes," a minute of supertime being the time it takes for the secondhand on "God's wristwatch" to traverse 360°.

direction and the possible world in which the rate of A-changes is zero. A reason for rejecting as spurious the latter is that if it were genuine, it's hard to see why a world with the A-changes taking place at a rate that was close to zero wouldn't be possible. But this the immediately preceding argument rules out. A reason for thinking the former possible world is a spurious one is that if it were not, it is difficult to see how we could be sure that it isn't, for all we know, the actual world. *Ex hypothesi,* the world in question is indistinguishable from the actual world in everything except the direction of A-changes. So everything that happens in it—excepting A-changes—is indiscernible from whatever happens in the actual world: all our thoughts and feelings are the same, they occur in the same order, and so forth. But if anything is clear, it is clear that Christmas 1990 is not receding from the present and Kennedy's assassination getting steadily closer to the present. Hence, the possible world in which A-changes occur in the opposite direction is not a genuine world.[9]

But if the foregoing considerations are sound, it follows that the doctrine of passage is false and hence that there just are no A-facts, notwithstanding deep-going intuitions to the contrary.

A closely related line of argument against the doctrine of passage also turns upon the "queerness" of the kinds of changes it appears to involve. Changes of the kind that allegedly occur when, say, an event like Lincoln's assassination recedes further and further into the past or a date like Christmas 1999 gets closer and closer to the present are not causally connected with any other events that take place in the world; nor, of course, is it ever necessary to appeal to them to explain anything that happens in the world. (These points will be the same if the notions of causality and explanation are properly analyzed in a certain way.) But (ostensible) changes that are in this way, this argument runs, disconnected from the rest of the world cannot fail to be at least suspect. Again, everything would be exactly the same whether they were there or not—everything that can be empirically detected, anyway. Thus, such changes are like wheels whose turning plays no role whatever in the operations of the mechanism of which they are a part. It's hard to believe that a complete and correct description of reality would refer to wheels of this kind, any more than it would refer to the actions/interactions of angels, fairies, or (for that matter) bits of antimatter if they were similarly causally isolated or explanatorily nugatory.[10]

Still another argument against the doctrine of passage runs thus. If the doctrine were true, then facts concerning the A-characteristics of things (so-called tensed facts) determine the truth-values of tokens of A-sentences, sentences like 'Event *e* happened five years ago' (S). After all, the truth of the doctrine entails the existence of such A-facts —such as the fact that *e* occurred five years ago; and if such facts are real features of the world, how could they fail to be the states of affairs that make tokens of sentences like S true, when they are true? But, the argument then continues, it is just false, and obviously false, that (alleged) facts of the kind in question determine the truth-values of tokens of A-sentences. Consider a token of S—call it 'S_{tk}'. Clearly S_{tk} is true if and only if the date of *e* is five years earlier than the date of S_{tk}. Similarly, a token of 'It is now April 25, 1985' (S'_{tk}) is evidently true if and only if S'_{tk} is uttered (or inscribed) on April 25, 1985. And so on. Hence the doctrine of passage is false.

A slightly different (and more complex) version of the same line of thought might be expressed thus. Either the truth-conditions of tokens of A-sentences (and A-judgments) are timeless or they are not. That is, the states of affairs that render such sentences or judgments true (or the obtaining of which make them true) when they are true, are either states of affairs that hold once and for all, or they are states of affairs that hold only temporarily, hold at some times and not at others. But if they are timeless, then the ostensible existence of A-facts is an illusion. After all, if there are such things as A-facts, how could they fail to constitute the facts that render tokens of A-sentences and A-judgments true, when they are true? On the other hand, if the truth-conditions of tokens of A-sentences and A-judgments are not timeless, then we seem forced to accept as true what seems upon reflection clearly false. Imagine that our Rip* in 1900, being quite disoriented, said to himself before falling into his long slumber, "It is now 1950." Then if A-facts constitute the truth-conditions of (tokens of) A-sentences and judgments, his judgment then was false, but later became true. For when he judged that it was 1950 (viz., in 1900 we are imagining) the fact of its now being 1950 did not obtain. But in 1950, of course, it did. So when the later date was present his earlier judgment became true, since then (in 1950) its truth-condition was satisfied. But it is surely false that Rip*'s mistaken 1900 judgment that it was then 1950 could become true. What he judged, after all—without knowing it, of course—was that the year 1900 was the year 1950. He thought, "It's now 1950," and 'now' picked out the year that was then elapsing: that's obviously how temporal indicator words like 'now' function. So what he judged was just false—and not just temporarily false, but eternally false. So the existence of A-facts has to be an illusion, and *a fortiori* the doctrine of passage false.[11]

IV

Considerations like those in the foregoing two sections bring out one of the central ways in which the idea of time gives rise to perplexity. Can this perplexity be dissolved by further reflection? Not perhaps in a way that is fully satisfactory. But we can at least make clear what we have to accept and what give up if we are to avoid embracing obviously unacceptable consequences. I shall begin the task of finding the least unsatisfactory view in this area by first scrutinizing the arguments in support of the doctrine of passage with an eye to seeing what their rejection commits us to. As we shall see, most can be rejected without our being committed to any theses that appear obviously suspect. One, however, we can reject only at what appears to be a substantial cost, but further reflection will show that cost to be minimal. For each of the arguments in question I shall first present a valid, although somewhat schematic, version of the argument. Then I shall indicate what I take to be its central flaw or flaws.

Argument A

1. We understand and know to be true many (tokens of) sentences like 'JFK's assassination is steadily moving further into the past'.
2. If 1, then there are A-facts.
3. If there are A-facts, then the doctrine of passage is true.

Therefore,

4. The doctrine of passage is true.

The first premise of Argument A is not a proposition many will wish to deny and the third is evidently true by virtue of the sense I have given to the expression 'A-facts'[12] and the content of the doctrine in question. It appears, then, that if we are to escape the force of this argument, we shall have to find reason to question its second premise. That is not difficult to do. Consider an A-sentence like 'JFK's death occurred 22 years ago'. What do we understand when we understand such a sentence? We understand what someone would be saying if she were, in certain circumstances, to utter the sentence—for example, that JFK's death occurred in 1963 if the sentence were uttered this year (I write this in 1985), and that JFK's death occurred in 1961 if the sentence were uttered in 1983. But if this is right, our understanding of the sentence provides no basis at all for believing in the existence of A-facts in the relevant sense. Similarly, what we know to be true when we know that a particular token of such a sentence is true is the truth of the proposition the token expresses in the circumstances of its issuance—for example, that JFK died in 1963. But again this fact yields no support for premise 2 of Argument A either. In short, the understanding and knowledge to which premise 2 alludes neither entails the existence of A-facts, nor requires the postulation of such facts if the existence of such understanding and knowledge is to be explained.

Argument B

1. The past is unalterable and (to a large extent) knowable in principle; the future is alterable and (to a large extent) unknowable in principle.
2. If 1, then the doctrine of passage is true.

Therefore,

3. The doctrine of passage is true.

Argument B is also easily withstood. The difficulty here is twofold. One problem is whether the past and future do differ in the respects indicated, and the other problem is whether any of the genuine differences between the past and the future are incompatible with the falsity of the doctrine of passage—appearances to the contrary notwithstanding. Let us consider first the claim that the future is alterable in a way that the past is not. Is it true, for example, that the past is unalterable in the sense that there is nothing we can do now to bring it about that

some fact about the past did not obtain? Not really. Suppose by
'Q-action' is meant an official action that plays a causal role in bringing
it about that nuclear weapons never come to be possessed by more
than, say, eight nations. Then the fact that a Q-action was performed
by the U.S. Senate when the nonproliferation treaty was ratified is not
"unalterable": we can, after all, do things now that will ensure that
such an action was not then performed—for example, make nuclear
weapons freely available to all members of the United Nations. Putting
aside such "soft" facts—facts the holding of which entails the occurrence or nonoccurrence of certain later events[13]—the past is normally
thought unalterable. There is certainly a firm intuition that there is
absolutely nothing we can do now to bring about that, for example,
Lincoln was not assassinated. Holding this, however, seems to amount
to nothing more than holding that no present actions could have any
effect on any non-soft fact about the past. Question: do the past and
the future differ as regards "alterability" in this sense? The answer
would appear to be "Yes" if backward causation is impossible and
"No" otherwise. Philosophers differ on this issue.[14] But in either case,
Argument B cannot be salvaged insofar as it turns on this idea of
alterability. For if backward causation is possible, the alleged alterability difference between the past and the future premise 1 asserts
dissolves. And if it isn't possible, with the result that only the future is
alterable, the difference will obviously be compatible with the absence
of A-facts. Lines of causal influence, after all, could run in only one
direction even if there were no changes of the kind the doctrine of
passage asserts.

Moreover, the alleged difference between the present and the future
as regards knowability in principle fares no better. On one interpreta-
tion of what this difference amounts to, it's not obvious that it exists.
Thus, suppose what it is for facts or objects to be "there to be known"
is just that a statement which states the alleged fact or says something
about the alleged object is true. Then it seems that the past and the
future do not really differ as regards "knowability in principle." It is,
after all, hard to deny that, for any intelligible future-tense statement
(as for any intelligible past-tense statement) either it is true or its
negation is true. Suppose *a* said that Ronald Reagan will die on
Christmas Day 1999 (call this statement 'S'). Now it's certainly plausible to hold that if Ronald Reagan does die on Christmas Day 1999,
then it will be the case then that S was true. But if it will be the case
then that S was true, how could it fail to be the case now that S is true?
Moreover, a similar point applies to not-S. But, we want to say, Ronald

Reagan will die on Christmas Day 1999 or he won't. So it follows that either S is (now) true or not-S is (now) true. If this is right, however, the idea that bivalence holds for past-tense statements cannot be used to explicate the alleged difference between the past and the future in question, since it appears also to hold for future-tense statements. And the only alternative way that comes to mind to explicate the alleged difference appeals to the idea that knowledge requires causal connections with the facts known, and causal influence runs only from earlier to later and not the other way round. Thus it might be said that the sense in which the past is knowable in principle is just that causal influence streams from the past to the present of a kind that makes knowledge of past events possible, at least in principle; and in this sense the future is obviously not knowable in principle since nothing that will occur exerts causal influence on the present. But again that backward causation is impossible is not obvious without argument. And, in any case, even if explicating the alleged "knowability in principle" difference in this way were successful, it would not serve to render the second premise of Argument B plausible for the reason noted at the end of the previous paragraph.

Argument C

1. If the doctrine of passage is false, then the future is as determinate as the past.
2. But if the future is as determinate as the past, then fatalism is true.
3. But fatalism is false.

Therefore,

4. The doctrine of passage is true.

It is the implausibility of premise 2 that renders this argument impotent. It's true that if the future is determinate, each of us has a complete biography in the sense that for each of us there is a collection of propositions that completely describes his or her life, past, present, and future. But the idea that the existence of such a complete biography entails that no one can do anything other than what he or she does do appears to rest upon a confusion. Suppose my complete biography contains the proposition *Robert Coburn flies to Denver on Christmas Day 1991*. Now why would anyone think that this fact entails that I cannot fail to fly to Denver then? Only, it would seem, by confusing the following two quite different propositions:

P □ (my complete biography contains *Robert Coburn flies to Denver on Christmas Day 1991* ⊃ Robert Coburn flies to Denver on Christmas Day 1991).

Q My complete biography contains *Robert Coburn flies to Denver on Christmas Day 1991* ⊃ □ Robert Coburn flies to Denver on Christmas Day 1991.

For P is obviously true; so if P were confused with Q one might think Q true. And the truth of propositions like Q is just what makes premise 2 of Argument C tempting. After all, if it is a necessary truth that I will fly to Denver on Christmas Day 1991, then there is no possibility that I won't. And if there is no possibility that I won't, then obviously I can't fail to do it. Moreover, the confusion of P and Q is easily made since the same form of words can be used to express both, viz., the sentence 'If my complete biography contains the proposition *Robert Coburn flies to Denver on Christmas Day 1991,* then it has to be true that (or it is necessarily the case that) I fly to Denver on Christmas Day 1991'. But obviously the existence of complete biographies sanctions P only, not Q. The mere fact, if it is a fact, that my complete biography contains the proposition in question—and hence that I will fly to Denver on Christmas Day 1991—is perfectly compatible with there being possible worlds in which I don't, or alternatively with it's being false that it is a necessary truth that I will fly to Denver then.

To be sure, if 'can't' is taken in a sense such that (or taken in such a way that) it's true that I can't do anything that falsifies a proposition in my complete biography, premise 2 of Argument C will hold. But then premise 3 will lose its plausibility. For it will then certainly not be obviously false that we can't do anything other than we do do so long as 'can't' carries its new sense—a sense, incidentally, that seems to be just the sense in which I can't assassinate JFK even if, perhaps *per impossibile,* I could travel backward in time to Dallas 1963.

Argument D

1. If the doctrine of passage is false, then the future is as determinate as the past.
2. If the future is as determinate as the past, then the full truth about

the world can be stated in a way that involves ascribing to things only properties that they possess "omnitemporally."
3. If the full truth about the world can be stated in a way that involves ascribing to things only properties that they possess "omnitemporally," then nothing ever really changes; change is an illusion.
4. It is false that change is an illusion.

Therefore,

5. The doctrine of passage is true.

Premises 1 and 4 of Argument D are difficult to fault. Premise 1 holds because rejecting the doctrine of passage involves rejecting a nonrelative distinction between past and future. Premise 4 is based upon one of our firmest intuitions about the world. Premise 2, on the other hand, may appear to some a shade less obvious. But if the idea of a complete and correct description of reality is acceptable, it too will, I think, appear at least quite plausible. Accordingly, the most attractive objection to this argument involves, I submit, rejecting its third premise.

Why is rejection of premise 3 plausible? Because the fact that the full truth about the world can be stated in a way that involves ascribing to things only properties that they possess "omnitemporally" is quite compatible with the reality of change—at least as we ordinarily understand what the reality of change requires. Consider what happens when my car undergoes a change as a result of being repainted or smashed in an accident. On Tuesday it was blue, and on Wednesday, green. Surely a genuine change has occurred; my car has changed color. But this fact is in no way impugned by the truth that my car's time-indexed properties are possessed by it throughout its career; that it never gains nor loses any of these properties; and indeed that the full truth about my car can be expressed by a complex set of propositions none of which involves reference to any properties that it (logically) could gain or lose during its career.

Moreover, if someone were to feel (or show) that the change in my car from being blue to being green is not (a case of) "genuine" change and that "genuine" change occurs only provided either (a) changes of the kind the doctrine of passage asserts occur, or (b) nothing really possesses now or in the past properties of the form $x[x$ has P at $t]$, where t is later than the present, or (c) both, then he (or one) could plausibly doubt, I submit, that premise 4 of Argument D *is* true. At any rate, it certainly won't be obvious without a powerful argument that this premise is true when it is construed in accordance with the above understanding of what the existence of "genuine" change requires.

Argument E

1. If the doctrine of passage is false, there are no A-facts and no fugitive propositions.
2. If there are no A-facts and no fugitive propositions, the truth-conditions of A-sentences are timeless and the propositions they express, eternal.
3. If the truth-conditions of A-sentences are timeless and the propositions they express eternal, A-sentences can be translated by eternal sentences, sentences whose truth-values never change.
4. But it is false that A-sentences can be translated by eternal sentences.

Therefore,

5. The doctrine of passage is true.

The problem with this argument does not lie with its first premise. If there were A-facts (and corresponding fugitive propositions), the doctrine of passage would be true: this is, in effect, what it asserts. Nor does it lie with premise 4. 'Today is May 1, 1985' clearly does not have an eternal sentence translation (that is, no sentence-type that, if true, is always true and, if false, is always false counts as a translation of the sentence-type in question). It lies rather with premises 2 and 3. Consider premise 2. It will be true if it refers to sentence-tokens but not if it refers to sentence-types. Thus, the absence of A-facts and fugitive propositions does ensure that the truth-conditions of tokens of sentences like 'Today is May 1, 1985' (S) are timeless (and the propositions they express eternal). For in the absence of A-facts and fugitive propositions, what could the truth-conditions of a token of S—S_{tk}, say—be if not that S_{tk} occurs on May 1, 1985; and that state of affairs is obviously one that holds timelessly, if it holds at all. On the other hand, if the reference in premise 2 is to sentence-types, then the premise fails because in the absence of A-facts and fugitive propositions, A-sentence-types will simply lack truth-conditions. In short, these sentence-types will be in the same semantic category with sentences like 'Your car is here' and 'I have a headache': such sentences as types are neither true nor false since what the singular terms they contain refer to is a function of the context of their utterance or inscription. But now on the reading of premise 2 on which it comes out true (the sentence-token-reading), premise 3 is clearly false. Even if the truth-conditions of A-sentence-tokens are timeless, that would not ensure that such tokens could be translated by eternal sentences; in other words, that there are sentence-types such that (a) if true they are always true and if false always false and (b) every token of an A-sentence—such as a token of 'Today is May 1, 1985' uttered at, say, *t*—can be translated by such a sentence-type. After all, if S_{tk} were synonymous with some eternal sentence—S_E, say—how could it fail to be true that any token of the type of which S_{tk} is a token could also be rendered by S_E—which would make S itself an eternal sentence. Or, to put the matter in another way, suppose there were an eternal sentence-type that translated S_{tk}—call it S_E. Then any token of S_E would be true if S_{tk} were true, no matter when this token were issued. But obviously there is no sentence-type that meets this condition.

Argument F

1. Whenever a person entertains a proposition or judges that a proposition is true or false, what proposition she entertains or judges to be true or false is determined by her mental (or brain) state at the time, a state as to the existence and character of which she is in an epistemically privileged position.
2. If premise 1 is true, then there exist fugitive propositions (and a fortiori A-facts).
3. If there exist fugitive propositions (and a fortiori A-facts), then the doctrine of passage is true.

Therefore,

4. The doctrine of passage is true.

So far all the arguments considered can be rejected, in my judgment, without incurring any serious costs or involving ourselves in metaphysical commitments of a kind that would be regarded as prima facie questionable by reasonable people without philosophical axes to grind. With Argument F, however, we reach an argument whose rejection does involve acceptance of a view that clearly flies in the face of the philosophical tradition, viz., the view that persons are *not* in an especially authoritative position to say what propositions they are currently entertaining, questioning, examining, judging to be true, etc. This is so because premises 2 and 3 of Argument F appear unassailable, with the result that the argument can be rejected only by rejecting its first premise. Yet a number of considerations can be adduced to make abandonment of the traditional view seem the best course quite independent of those that are designed specifically to overthrow the doctrine of passage. Thus, suppose we accept that Rip* believes different propositions right before he falls asleep and when he awakens 50 years later. Then we shall need a different way of describing what it is that the mental states of Rip^*_{1900} and Rip^*_{1950} have in common. John Perry has suggested we say that Rip^*_{1900} and Rip^*_{1950} "accept" the same sentence, viz., the sentence 'It is now 1990', where to accept a sentence containing indicator words like 'now' is (a) to believe whatever proposition a token-utterance of (or token-judgment involving) that sentence expresses in the context of its occurrence, and (b) to be in a state that is self-intimating and that plays the role in the explanation of behavior traditionally assigned to belief thought of as an unmediated relation of a subject to a proposition.[15] Once we think in this way about our relation to A-sentences and the propositions tokens of these sentences express under different circumstances, however, we can give illuminating accounts of some phenomena that are quite baffling on the traditional view. First, we can explain our inclination to think that Rip* believed something false in 1950, even though he believed something true in 1900 and (as we think) had not changed his mind. We can say that he believed different propositions on the two occasions—one true and one false—because what proposition a person believes in virtue of accepting an A-sentence like 'It is now 1900' depends upon the context in which the token appears. And we can explain our inclination to say his mind hadn't changed because he was in the same belief-state (that is, he accepted the same sentence) on the two occasions. Second, we can similarly explain our inclination in certain situations to say that two persons have and yet fail to have the same beliefs. Thus suppose A and B both accept the sentence 'I am the tallest man in the world'. We could say that A and B believe the same thing insofar as they are in the same belief-state. Yet we could also hold that they believe different things, since the proposition A believes in virtue of being in this belief-state is different from the proposition B believes in virtue of his being in this belief-state. We can even make sense of an inclination in a certain type of case to say that A and B have the same belief about A and yet still have different beliefs. Suppose A and B each thinks he is A and that each accepts the sentence 'I am the tallest man in the world' (S). Then they would share not only a belief-state, but they would both believe the proposition that A is the tallest man in the world. Still, we'd want to say that they have different beliefs. The explanation of this would be that B, in virtue of accepting S, would also hold true the proposition that B was the tallest man in the world, a proposition A would not believe in virtue of accepting S.

We do, then, have to abandon the traditional way of thinking about what it is to believe and entertain propositions if we reject Argument F. But the cost of doing so is negligible or less, I suggest, given the independent reason that can be provided for thinking the traditional view unacceptable anyway.

Argument G

1. We have and express attitudes whose "objects" are A-facts.
2. If premise 1 is true, then A-facts exist.
3. If A-facts exist, the doctrine of passage is true.

Therefore,

4. The doctrine of passage is true.

Once we have at hand this notion of a belief-state, a plausible way of rejecting premise 1 of Argument G is not far to seek. We can generalize the notion to encompass all the so-called propositional attitudes and then conceive of the state a person expresses when he issues a token of a sentence like 'I'm glad *e* is over' as a state that consists in a certain attitude toward an A-sentence and through it toward the state of affairs that is expressed by that sentence in the context in which the token occurs. If, for example, a person says "I'm glad *e* is over" at 9:00 P.M. EST on May 1, 1990, what he is glad about is that *e* occurred earlier than 9:00 P.M. EST, May 1, 1990. But, and this is the crucial point, the speaker may not know that this is the state of affairs toward which his attitude is directed. He may know only that the state of affairs he is glad about is expressed by the A-sentence he uses in expressing his attitude, given the context in which his use of that sentence occurs—whatever its relevant features may be. And it is this fact that he may be ignorant of what state of affairs it is toward which his attitude is directed—although of course he does know that it is the unique state of affairs that satisfies a certain description (viz., "the state of affairs that is expressed by an utterance of sentence S now")—which explains our inclination to deny that what we're glad about when we're glad some painful experience (say) is over is that the experience is timelessly earlier than some specific date and which explains *a fortiori* our temptation to accept premise 1 of Argument G.

It's possible, of course, that at least some attitude-expressions of the kind in question encapsulate the picture of time the doctrine of passage involves. I'm inclined to think this is probably true of remarks like "I wish it were now 1930," for example. That is, it's most plausible to suppose that a person who says something like this is, as it were, imaginatively taking up a perspective outside of time, viewing the A-series with its continuously changing A-facts and wishing that the A-facts that hold now were different in certain ways from what they are. If this is right, then the generalization of Perry's account of believing to other propositional attitudes won't suffice by itself to undercut the argument for premise 2 of Argument G. We shall also have to accept the idea that some of our talk embodies the view the arguments we are now discussing seek to establish, and the rejection of at least one of these arguments requires conceding that some of the things we say make sense only against the background of a metaphysical theory that may well turn out to be quite unacceptable, all things considered.

V

It seems, then, that none of the arguments presented in section II in favor of the doctrine of passage is very persuasive. One might suppose that this implies that the arguments against the doctrine are sound, but such an inference would be invalid. The failure of the arguments in question does not entail that there are no good arguments for the doctrine of passage. And even if there aren't, it wouldn't follow either that the doctrine is false or that any of the arguments given in support of such a conclusion are sound. Still, the failure of the arguments for the doctrine that we have considered does provide some reason for supposing that there may well be good arguments against it. I consider now whether any of the arguments presented in section III count as arguments of this sort.

The first of these arguments against the doctrine of passage, it will be recalled, went in outline as follows:

Argument H

1. If the doctrine of passage were true, then there are possible worlds w, w' and w'' exactly like the actual world except that (a) in w A-changes take place at a different rate, (b) in w' they take place in the opposite direction, and (c) in w'' A-changes do not take place at all.
2. There are no such possible worlds.

Therefore,

3. The doctrine of passage is false.

What makes premise 1 of this argument plausible is a certain conception of what the doctrine of passage asserts. In other words, premise 1 is plausible only if it is taken as a partial explication of what the truth of the doctrine involves. Unfortunately, when it is understood in this way, it is less than obvious, I submit, that the possible worlds that have to exist if the doctrine is true are spurious. Why should it not be true, for example, that there is a possible world exactly like ours in which A-changes take place in the opposite direction—indeed, that our world might be such a world? On the other hand, if one thinks it is perfectly evident that there are no such worlds, that the idea of possible worlds exactly like ours except for lacking A-changes lacks clear sense, then it may well not seem obvious that the doctrine of passage requires the existence of such worlds. Why should it not be the case instead that A-changes come in only one form, so to speak, or that the idea of such changes is wrongly construed on the model of changes that take place at some rate that could have been otherwise or that could take place in the opposite direction? In any case, in the absence of a strong argument to the effect that the idea of such a *sui generis* change is unintelligible, premise 1 of Argument H remains doubtful at best.[16]

The second of the arguments presented against the doctrine of passage can be schematically stated thus.

Argument I

1. If the doctrine of passage is true, A-changes exist.
2. But A-changes are causally isolated and explanatorily nugatory—disconnected from the rest of the mechanism, so to speak.
3. If premise 2 is true, A-changes are not genuine changes.

Therefore,

4. The doctrine of passage is false.

There is no basis for disputing premises 1 and 2 of this argument. But premise 3 is less obvious, I think. Why should it be true, one wants to ask, that changes of the kind that are part and parcel of the metaphysical structure of the world should have the same status as do empirical changes that take place "within" the world—and which presuppose this structure? We might legitimately deny the genuineness of changes that are (allegedly) part of empirical reality if their postulation (or recognition) were not required by what we take to be the best overall explanatory theory of the way things (empirically) go. But this fact in no way impugns features of the world that are built into its categorical structure unless that structure is also to be read off the best overall scientific theory of the way things go. But it's at least plausible to hold that it isn't, to hold, for example, that the categorical structure of reality is presupposed by the very practice of evidence-gathering and theory-formation upon which empirical science rests. Such a view may be mistaken, but if so it is not obviously mistaken. And because of this Argument I as it stands is hardly coercive.[17]

The third argument, which came in two slightly different versions, can be set out as follows:

Argument J

1. If the doctrine of passage is true, then there are A-facts.
2. If there are A-facts, then they determine the truth-values of tokens of A-sentences.
3. It is false that A-facts determine the truth-values of tokens of A-sentences.

Therefore,

4. The doctrine of passage is false.

Argument J*

1. Either the truth-conditions of tokens of A-sentences are timeless or they are not.
2. If they are timeless, then the ostensible existence of A-facts is an illusion.
3. If they are not timeless, then, provided event e occurred five years ago, any token of the sentence 'e happened five years ago' will be true regardless of the date of its occurrence.
4. It is false that any token of such a sentence is true regardless of the date of its occurrence.

Therefore,

5. The doctrine of passage is false.

Unlike Arguments H and I, these arguments seem to me quite coercive. If Argument J is to be faulted, obviously it will have to be premise 3 that is rejected, and if Argument J* is unsound, it will have to be premise 4 that is false. Both, however, are very difficult to reject, and for the same reason. The truth-values of tokens of A-sentences seem on the face of it to be of the sort I indicated above, following Mellor (see section III). After all, if we give up this view of the truth-conditions of such token-sentences we have to say, for example, that a token of '*e* occurred five years ago' could be true even though it occurs before *e*, which seems just wildly wrong. We also have to say that the proposition this token expresses at the time of its utterance is a proposition that comes to be true at a later time. But that, too, is very hard to accept. Surely the proposition we express when, at t $(t<e)$, we utter a token of '*e* occurred five years ago' is false and remains false, and this despite the fact that when someone utters a token of this sentence-type at t^* (where t^* is five years after t), the proposition she thereby expresses is true. Denying this would be tantamount to holding that when A, speaking in Detroit, utters a token of 'Your book is here' (even though in fact it's in Chicago), the proposition A expresses is *true in Chicago!*

If a plausible case could be made for denying that there is any such thing as "the actual future course of events," of course, then the Mellorian account of the truth-conditions of tokens of A-sentences could not be correct. For on this account, a token of 'Comet *c* will return 50 years hence' (S_{tk}) is true if and only if *c* returns 50 years after the occurrence of S_{tk}. So if S_{tk} occurs in 1985, its truth entails that there is an actual future course of events and that it contains the return of *c* 50 years later. But the only ways I can see of developing this idea are, on the face of it, quite hopeless. For consider. An advocate of such a view will have to say something like the following. A "possible world" consists of "the actual present state and the past history of the world, together with some complete possible history of it."[18] Moreover, reality simply consists of the set of possible worlds in this sense, a set that continually diminishes with the passage of time; and the idea of there being a set of (nonrelatively) true propositions about reality is given up in favor of the thought that propositions are true (or false) only in possible worlds, that is, only relative to given possible worlds.

Such a conception seems hard to reconcile with current physical theory, however, since current theory is ostensibly incompatible with the idea of there being a nonrelative distinction between what is future and what is present or past.[19] Also, it is strongly counterintuitive to deny that future-tense token-sentences uttered now are determinately true or false for reasons of a kind indicated in section IV above.

VI

Accepting the soundness of Arguments J and J*, and *a fortiori* the falsity of the doctrine of passage, is not, as noted earlier, without its costs. I shall now consider what these are and what, if anything, can be said by way of mitigating them.

Giving up the doctrine of passage does not require, of course, that we give up saying that some times, objects, and events are past, some present, and some future. But it does require that we concede that items are past, present, and future only relative to the temporal positions of other such items and that the contents of the present (or "the present-cum-past") are no more "real" than the contents of the future. Do such concessions count as serious costs of giving up the doctrine of passage?

It can, at first, certainly seem so. For we appear required to embrace the idea that if, *per impossibile,* we could shift the present forward or backward 400 years, say, the result would not be different in any way from what in fact obtains.[20] Alternatively, we are forced to admit that if there were an omniscient God who transcended the natural order, the order of things in space and time, he would not be missing anything if all he knew about temporal matters were propositions that described such unchanging facts as that $e_1 < e_2$, $e_2 < e_3$, and so on. In particular, if all he knew were propositions about the natures and relative (spatial and temporal) positions of things and events, he wouldn't fail to know what is going on now (or what year is currently elapsing).[21] Or suppose we let 'e_1' name the event of Ronald Reagan's signing a certain bill today, 'e_2' name the event of Ronald Reagan's birth, and 'e_3' the event of Ronald Reagan's death. Then if we give up the doctrine of passage, we have to hold that there is no sense in which e_1 has a different ontological status from e_2 and e_3; we have to hold that, in a tenseless sense of the verb 'to occur', e_1, e_2, and e_3 are all occurring, although to be sure at different times.

Counterintuitive as these consequences of the doctrine's rejection may at first appear, their sting can be softened by considerations like the following: (1) First, although it's true that e_2 and e_3 are occurring in the tenseless sense of this verb, this seems paradoxical only, I suspect, because of a tendency to understand 'occurring' in such statements as tensed and so as meaning the same as 'occurring now'. One way of protecting against this tendency is to explicate the tenseless sense of 'is occurring' as meaning "occurred in the past, is occurring now, or will occur in the future," and then to use that explication in formulating the thesis in question. No one, I take it, doubts that e_3 "is occurring," where this means it occurred in the past, is occurring now, or will occur in the future.

(2) The feeling that God would be missing something crucial if all he knew were facts about the various B-series (see section 1) is not as easily handled. But these points at least can be made. First, the idea of God the puzzle turns on is not obviously intelligible. Could there be something that did not exist in time and yet was capable of knowing things? Second, even if we are unable to bring ourselves to a state of confidence on this question, it remains that such a being would be missing something only if the doctrine of passage is true. So any reasons for rejecting that doctrine are *eo ipso* reasons for doubting that such a being would fail to know all there is to be known. It seems, then, that the consequences in question will count as a cost for one who rejects the doctrine of passage only to the extent (a) that he is inclined to think a certain picture of God could have application and, in addition, (b) that he feels tempted to say that God would be missing something after he has given full weight to the considerations that fuel Arguments J and J*.

(3) Finally, the following may be said about the shifting-the-present paradox. The kind of shift the paradox turns on does not seem to represent a logical possibility, and this even if the doctrine of passage is assumed true. And if it could be shown that it was, given the truth of the doctrine of passage, why wouldn't this argument itself count against the doctrine of passage and hence the seriousness of the cost this puzzle allegedly involves? Moreover, the very idea of such a shift presupposes the doctrine of passage. This is so because it presupposes an absolute distinction between past, present, and future of just the kind the doctrine involves. For this reason, it's hard to see how the feeling that such a shift would change things could plausibly count in favor of the doctrine and so count as a cost for those who reject it.

Despite considerations like the foregoing, a certain vague disquietude may continue to accompany abandonment of the doctrine of passage. I suspect the best way of removing—or at least lessening—it is by uncovering the possible sources of our inclinations to embrace the doctrine other than those that underlie the arguments presented in section II. By way of conclusion, I shall indicate two such sources, exposure of which might help to counteract this deep-lying tendency in our thought.

First, there is the fact that accepting an A-sentence like 'I am now writing this page' (S) involves holding true in succession a number of quite different propositions. Thus, my accepting S at t_1 involves my holding true the proposition that I am writing this page at t_1; my accepting S at t_2 involves my holding true the proposition that I am writing this page at t_2; and so on. So my acceptance of S over an interval of time is correlated with an objective change, a change in the propositions I thereby hold true at different points in that interval. This fact might well help explain our tendency to believe in temporal passage. For it might be said that we have a natural tendency to confuse the objective change that accompanies the acceptance of such A-sentences over a period of time with the kind of change the doctrine of passage asserts.[22]

A second possible source of the tendency to embrace the doctrine of passage might be a natural tendency to picture time as a river, the objects and events that exist and take place in time as bits of flotsam and jetsam floating in it, and the present as a fixed point past which the river and its contents pass as they move from future to past. In any case, we can see how such a tendency might be native to the human mind—why shouldn't such intellectual dispositions be phenotypic expressions of the human gene pool?—and we can see that if it were, a doctrine like the doctrine of passage would be a natural outgrowth of it. Indeed, it might even be that belief in the doctrine itself is rooted in the genome, that the concept of time with which we prereflectively operate is an innate concept whose proper analysis involves both B-facts and A-facts. There is no solid evidence, of course, that either of these views is true. But we certainly don't know they are false. (Neither is incompatible, for example, with our being able to conceive of time along different lines.) So both are possible sources of the tendency to embrace the doctrine of passage, at least in the epistemic sense of 'possible'.

How far considerations like these go in removing the disquietude that may stand in the way of accepting the coerciveness of Arguments J and J* may well vary from person to person. I think they go a considerable distance. But I also suspect there may well be more to say on this matter. If the existence of A-facts is an illusion, it is one of our most stubborn ones. Its roots are probably as reticulate as they are deep.

Notes

1. That is, relative to any rigid body or collection of material objects that retain the same spatial relations among themselves over time. See Richard Swinburne, *Space and Time* (New York: St Martin's Press, 1968), chap. 1.

2. See J. M. E. McTaggart, *The Nature of Existence*, vol. 2 (Cambridge: Cambridge University Press, 1927), chap. 33.

3. For a given choice of interval (and "unit" of temporal distance), the present interval can be taken to be that interval the mid-point of which is contemporary with what is momentarily transpiring—relative to the frame of reference in question, of course.

4. I make use here of ideas presented in D. Lewis, "The Paradoxes of Time Travel," *American Philosophical Quarterly* 13 (1976).

5. D. H. Mellor speaks of such facts as "tensed facts" in *Real Time* (Cambridge: Cambridge University Press, 1980), chap. 6 and passim.

6. See, for example, Austin Duncan-Jones, "Fugitive Propositions," *Analysis* 10 (1949).

7. Cf. A. N. Prior, "Thank Goodness That's Over," *Philosophy* 34 (1959).

8. Cf. G. Schlesinger, *Aspects of Time* (Indianapolis: Hackett Publishing, 1980), p. 38 f.

9. The general features of this type of criticism of the doctrine of passage are quite familiar in the literature. See, for example, R. Taylor, *Metaphysics*, 3rd ed. (Englewood Cliffs: Prentice-Hall, 1983), chap. 8. The way I have developed the features, however, are my own.

10. This line of thought is suggested by A. Grünbaum, "The Status of Temporal Becoming," in R. Gale, ed., *The Philosophy of Time* (Garden City, N.Y.: Anchor, 1967); J. J. C. Smart, *Philosophy and Scientific Realism* (London: Routledge & Kegan Paul, 1963), chap. 7; and P. C. W. Davies, *Space and Time in the Modern Universe* (Cambridge: Cambridge University Press, 1977), p. 220 f. and passim.

11. The arguments in this and the preceding paragraph are due—in essence—to D. H. Mellor. See *Real Time*, chap. 6.

12. See Sec II above. Of course, in a sense there are facts that correspond to tokens of A-sentences, when these tokens are true. That is, it is correct to speak of the fact that today is August 3, 1988. Such facts are, as it were, the grammatical shadows of the tokens themselves. But the existence of A-facts in the sense in which the doctrine of passage asserts their existence does not follow from these "shadows." For A-facts in this sense exist only if these shadow-facts are irreducible. That is to say, only if each fact of the relevant

kind is such that its existence does *not consist in* the existence of one or more facts of some class the members of which can be expressed without using temporal indexicals.

13. This idea of a "soft" fact was first presented, to my knowledge, by Marilyn McCord Adams, in "Is the Existence of God a 'Hard' Fact?," *Philosophical Review* 76 (1967).

14. Proponents of backward causation include M. Dummett, "Bringing About the Past," *Philosophical Review* 73 (1964); R. Chisholm and R. Taylor, "Making Things to Have Happened," *Analysis* 20 (1960); and D. Lewis, "The Paradoxes of Time Travel," among others. Among those who argue against backward causation is D. H. Mellor. See *Real Time,* chap. 10.

15. See J. Perry, "Frege on Demonstratives," *Philosophical Review* 86 (1977); "The Problem of the Essential Indexical," *Nous* 13 (1979); and "Belief and Acceptance," in Peter A. French, Theodore E. Uehling, Jr., and Howard K. Wettstein, eds., *Midwest Studies in Philosophy,* vol. 5 (Minneapolis: University of Minnesota Press, 1980).

16. That such an idea of a *sui generis* change is not obviously unintelligible is suggested by the fact that a philosopher as acute as C. D. Broad embraced it. See his *An Examination of McTaggart's Philosophy,* Vol. 2 (Cambridge: Cambridge University Press, 1938), chap. 35.

17. The most important recent statement and defense of the Kantian view that scientific theory-confirmation presupposes a doctrine or view of the world that is not itself empirically confirmable is probably Wittgenstein's *On Certainty,* trans. D. Paul and G. E. M. Anscombe (Oxford: Basil Blackwell, 1969). But also very suggestive here is A. Donagan's "Realism and Freethinking in Metaphysics," *Theoria* 3 (1970).

18. M. Dummett, "Realism," *Synthese* 52 (1982): 88. The way of understanding the notion of possibility involved here is this: "a future event is possible if it does not follow from the present state of the world, taken together with the laws of nature, that it will not occur" (ibid.).

19. See H. Putnam, "Time and Physical Geometry," *Journal of Philosophy* 64 (1967). Although I should note that Lawrence Sklar in "Time, Reality and Relativity," in R. Healey, ed., *Reduction, Time and Reality* (Cambridge: Cambridge University Press, 1981) argues that relativity theory is strictly compatible with the views that only the present is real and that only the present-cum-past is real. However, he also makes clear that what one has to accept if one holds both that relativity theory is correct and that one or the other of these metaphysical views is true is unappetizing at best.

20. Cf. Mellor, *Real Time,* p. 28 f.

21. Cf. M. Dummett, "A Defense of McTaggart's Proof of the Unreality of Time," *Philosophical Review* 69 (1960): 501; and A. N. Prior, "The Formalities of Omniscience," *Philosophy* 37 (1962): 116.

22. This line of thought is suggested by Mellor, *Real Time,* p. 114 f.

CHAPTER SEVEN

Metaphysical Theology and the Life of Faith

I

Although perhaps less pervasive than some of the other ideas considered earlier in this book, the idea expressed by 'God' and its cognates occupies a prominent place in the thought and speech of large numbers of human beings. In the Judeo-Christian tradition,[1] this idea tends to be elaborated in two antithetical ways. On the one hand is a tendency to structure the concept so as to make it analytic that God is absolutely unlimited ("infinite"), that is, devoid of any feature(s) the possession of which would in any way restrict or define it, or distinguish it from anything else, actual or possible. This tendency, accordingly, leads to denials that God is a being who exists "alongside" others, a particular (or substance) that can enter into causal relations (or causally interact) with other things and that can be an object of knowledge. It even leads to the view that nothing can be said that is *literally* true of God other than perhaps that God is cognitively approachable only by the use of "symbolic expressions" that at best are less misleading than certain others.[2] (I shall hereafter refer to theological conceptions that give expression to this tendency as "mystical" or "negative" conceptions.)

The other and conflicting tendency expresses itself in the development of "anthropomorphic" (or "positive") conceptions of God, that is, conceptions according to which it is analytic that God is, for example, a determinate—although usually immaterial—particular who exists in and endures through time, is causally responsible for the existence and (at least some of the) operations of the things that exist other than himself, and possesses intentions and purposes, knowledge, and attitudes like love that are directed toward things other than himself. On some of these conceptions, God, like human beings, even lacks definitive knowledge of how things will go in the future, or is subject to limitations on his power that (even) go beyond those imposed by the laws of logic.[3]

Not infrequently, of course, both tendencies will be present in the mind of a religious thinker, with the result that he will either fall into contradiction or—perhaps unwittingly—present what I once referred to as a "barmecidal" theological conception.[4] That is, he will structure his concept of God in anthropomorphic terms at one stage in his presentation and perhaps later present an account of the nature of theological language that has the effect of quashing the possibility of taking the words he earlier used in developing his conception of God in a natural (or literal) way. He may say, for example, that although the most informative theological statements we can make (such as "God is good," "God is a person," "God created heaven and earth and all the things that dwell therein") are literally true, the meanings carried by the predicate expressions in question are, when so used, beyond our intellectual grasp, at least to a significant extent, and this despite the fact that we understand quite well what these expressions convey when applied to "finite" things.[5] Alternatively, he may insist that the most informative statements we can make about God are ineluctably nonliteral. He may talk of phrases like 'beyond the world' as conveying only a "model," since 'beyond' is used "analogically and not literally."[6] He may characterize theological assertions as "mythological" or "pictorial" and maintain that such myths or pictures are not susceptible of being cashed in literal terms.[7] He may characterize such statements as "parabolic" or as statements that present or convey "images," which parables or images can be "appropriate," or "true," even though the truth they express cannot be stated in any other way.[8]

These conflicting tendencies have many sources, as will later become clear. But at least one of the central of these lies in a concern to avoid the severe problems that appear to beset theological conceptions to which the opposing tendency leads. In the next section, I shall indicate some of the main problems in question and in so doing make clear, I hope, why the concept of God has seemed so problematic to many. Then I shall explore the question whether (and to what extent) the perplexity that lies at the heart of traditional metaphysical theology is inimical to the religious life. More specifically, I shall first set forth a plausible account of what "the life of faith" consists in. Then I shall consider the relation between traditional metaphysical theology and the life of faith. Finally, I shall make some remarks about the character and roles of the language used by the faithful to express and convey their religious attitudes and beliefs.

II

The reasons why the mystical (or negative) conceptions of God are problematic are of two kinds. First, these conceptions appear at best distressingly near to the boundary separating sense from nonsense; at worst they are well beyond the boundary. Suppose we understand an "individual" to be anything that can be an object of reference.[9] Then God will count as an individual, at least on the assumption that 'God' functions like an ordinary proper name (or a referring expression very like an ordinary proper name). Moreover, if we adopt the view that, excepting certain special cases, properties are expressed by open sentences in one free variable and hold that there are truths expressible by sentences in which 'God' functions as a genuine referring expression, then God clearly has properties. It would seem then that if we adopt certain common accounts of what individuals and properties are and accept the views of the faithful that 'God' is a genuinely referring expression and that there are truths about God, we cannot, on pain of contradiction, go on to hold that God "transcends" the distinction between individuals and properties. Again, if we define the complement of a property P as the property anything lacking P cannot fail to have, then any assertion that God can only be described negatively (that is, said not to be characterizable in such and such ways) is also contradictory. For any truth of the form 'God lacks property P' entails a truth of the form 'God possesses the complement of P'.

But suppose a theologian who is prone to think of God along mystical lines were to grant that God is an individual since there is a "reality" that is referred to by this use of the word 'God', and that this reality possesses certain properties, viz., the complements of those he feels confident we should deny of God. Will he then have a conception that is at least intelligible? That will depend; in particular, it will depend upon exactly what features he wants to deny of God. If, as those in the mystical tradition are prone to do, he insists that God is not a concrete particular that is distinct from, and that exists in addition to, the other things that exist, is not an entity that causes the other things that exist to exist, is not a property or relation or some other sort of abstract entity, and is not located in either space or time (perhaps among other things), then it is far from clear that his conception is an intelligible one. After all, told that there (really!) is an individual that is not a concrete particular nor an abstract entity, that occupies no place, that does not exist now nor at any other time, and that has no causal interactions with anything else, we shall certainly have little idea of what difference there is between accepting and rejecting the proposition that there is such an individual, and we shall certainly be baffled by anyone who claims to believe that there is such an individual. Nor, I suspect, will this bafflement be assuaged if that person goes on to say that this individual is (or has) perfect bliss, is alone really real, and is indistinguishable from "pure consciousness." For though these ideas may not at first glance appear vacuous, when combined with the other (negative) attributions, how they are to be understood is (at least) very difficult to grasp.[10]

Should the mystically inclined theologian seek to assuage our difficulties by talking of myths and metaphors, symbols and models, parables and pictures, insisting of course that what these manage to express cannot be conveyed in any other way, and in particular by the use of language that is to be understood in a literal and straightforward way, our understanding of his conception of God would not be much improved. For to be told that God is a loving father or that human history is in the hands of a providential agent working out his hidden purposes, and then that these words are not to be taken literally, is not to be told anything intelligible when such remarks are combined with thoughts of the kind noted in the preceding paragraph. How, after all, could anything that is timeless and incapable of causal interactions be even remotely like a loving father or a purposeful agent working his ways in human history?

These broadly logical difficulties are not the only ones that beset those who structure the concept of God along mystical (or negative) lines. There are, in addition, religious difficulties. Among the "spiritual" problems that give the great religious traditions their purchase on human life are (a) "the problem of guilt," (b) "the problem of death," and (c) "the problem of meaninglessness."[11] The first problem is felt by those who are burdened by a sense of having seriously failed to live up to the moral standards they have internalized—and preeminently by those for whom this burden is so heavy that they can endure life only by frantically seeking to distract their minds from the facts that give rise to their feelings of guilt. By the problem of death I have in mind the anguish that many feel at the thought of their own imminent or eventual extinction, as well as the deep disquietude that springs from all the present or probable future "slings and arrows" that strike us all as finite beings: illness and disabling accidents, missed opportunities, wasted time and energy, loss or disdain of loved ones, and the desirelessness and crippling incapacities of old age. The third problem, the problem of meaninglessness, is felt by all those who sense the pursuits and achievements of life to be "vanity," at core empty or hollow. It manifests itself in a deep sadness, in loss of zest for life, in cynicism, and—at its worst—in despair ("the sickness unto death"). The *loci classici* in which these three spiritual problems are powerfully expressed include Paul's letter to the Romans, the Book of Job, and the Book of Ecclesiastes.[12] If problems like these often lead people to religion, it is easy to understand why mystical conceptions of God may well be felt wanting. A person wracked by guilt may hunger for the forgiveness of one who knows all. But a God who is not a distinct being possessing familiar kinds of psychological features will not be a God capable of the requisite acts. Those plagued by the problems of death and meaninglessness have frequently felt the need for a more anthropomorphic deity as well. At any rate, the possibility of a desirable form of life after death and the existence of "objective meaningfulness" have often been connected in the minds of religious people with the existence of a very humanlike deity capable of bestowing immortality and bliss upon those he loves and capable of ensuring that our struggles and accomplishments are rescued from eternal oblivion by being (somehow) woven into a larger tapestry that serves some exalted extrahuman purpose.[13]

But if mystical conceptions possess serious liabilities, anthropomorphic conceptions fare no better. On these conceptions, God is typically conceived as a being who is distinct from and independent of the other things that exist, who possesses a very great—and perhaps unsurpassable—capacity to effect changes in the world, who possesses vast and detailed knowledge of the objects, events, and states of affairs that make up the world, and whose unwavering purposes include—perhaps inter alia—the well-being and happiness of creatures like us. Anthropomorphically inclined thinkers differ, however, on whether God should be thought of as eternal or temporal, necessary or contingent, and perfect or only "finitely perfect." And this no doubt is true because whatever decision is made on these issues gives rise to severe difficulties.

Thus, if such an anthropomorphic God is conceived as existing "outside of time" (eternal), it will be hard to maintain that he is (very like) a person, that is, the kind of being who can forgive sins, answer prayers, alter his decisions in the light of changing circumstances in order better to achieve his purposes, and so on. On the other hand, if he is conceived as existing in time (as sempiternal), it will be difficult to avoid thinking of him as contingent, as the sort of being who (logically) could have failed to exist. After all, if God exists in time as one existent among many, it is difficult to see that there is any contradiction involved in his ceasing to exist at some point in the future. But if God could cease to exist at some point in the future, that he exists now can hardly be necessary truth. But if God's existence is thus a contingent matter, his existence would seem to be "a grace of fate."[14] But such a God will be a less satisfactory target of religious emotions than one conceived as not liable to the winds of fortune. Such a God will also be unsatisfactory from the point of view of those who turn to religion for an answer to the question why anything exists at all. If God is just one more contingent being among the contingent beings that make up the world, the fact that he has created everything other than himself will, as has often been noted, in no way put to rest this question.[15]

A decision to hold that God's existence is necessary, however, does not help matters. In the first place, if it is true that anything that exists in time is contingent, this decision will carry with it the view that God is eternal and hence the liabilities this idea carries (mentioned above). In addition, the thesis that God's existence is necessary contradicts the firm intuitions of many that it is at least possible (a) that nothing should have existed and (b) that the only things that exist are their own present experiences. Third, this decision to conceive of God as a necessary being generates the following dilemma. If God is thought of as both omnipotent and perfectly good, either God's possession of these properties is also necessary or it is not. If it isn't, then the world could have been such that God existed but was very limited in power and not at all good, a Charles Manson sort of person perhaps. But, again, many religious people will insist that anything of which this is true is not a worthy object of worship. Also, it is hard to see how God's existence could be necessary if, in some worlds, he is an object of this kind. On the other hand, if God's existence is necessary and God possesses omnipotence and perfect goodness necessarily too, then he possesses these characteristics in every possible world. But then God's existence is contradictory, at least on a natural understanding of what omnipotence and perfect goodness involve. For to be omnipotent, one naturally thinks, is to be able to do many horrible things even in the absence of adequate justification, and to be able to do things one does not in fact do is just for there to be a (non-actual) possible world in which one does these things. But if God is perfectly good in every possible world in which he exists and he exists in every possible world, then there is no possible world in which God does horrible things without adequate justification. Hence it is impossible that God should necessarily exist and, in addition, possess omnipotence and perfect goodness necessarily.

Then too, if God is conceived as perfect in knowledge, power, and goodness, the existence of the kinds and amount of evil that the world contains becomes very difficult to understand. Even if some of this evil is explainable as due to the free actions of human beings, and much of the rest is explainable by reference to the free actions of nonhuman created spirits of some sort, it is still hard to see why so much is permitted when God knows how it could be stopped, his power is sufficient to limit it, and his goodness of a sort that would seem to require that he act on his knowledge. Solving this problem by denying that God's knowledge, power, and goodness are without limits also has its costs. Once again, a finitely perfect God appears to many not to be an adequate object of worship.

Finally, all anthropomorphic conceptions are liable to an epistemological problem that mystical conceptions avoid, insofar anyhow as they are unintelligible. There seem to be no reasons for thinking God exists when so conceived, at least reasons that generate arguments that command the assent of any reasonable person who is capable of understanding them and appreciating their force.[16] This problem is especially acute if it is also true, as is plausibly maintained, that a person can believe a proposition only if he thinks it to be more probable than any alternative.[17] For in that case, not only will belief in God be unsupportable, it will also be impossible—at least for those apprised of the epistemological status of the proposition that God exists. But even if belief in God is possible for those who are aware of the absence of adequate reason for thinking that he exists, this epistemological situation is an unsatisfactory one insofar as metaphysico-theological belief plays a significant role in determining how a person lives his or her life. A person cannot but be deeply disturbed by the fact that his or her life is built on a foundation of sand.

III

Metaphysical theology, it seems, is rife with problems. Many take this to show that the religious life is problematic at best, since it seems to rest upon a foundation of metaphysical theology; at any rate, it appears to do so if our paradigms of the religious life are drawn from the Christian, Jewish, or Muslim traditions. On the face of it, these religions rest on metaphysical foundations, so how could the piety, faith, or spirituality of their adherents fail to do so, too? When one considers in detail what "the life of faith" involves, however, this conclusion appears somewhat off the target. The proper formulation of the relation of religiosity and metaphysical theology is both more complicated and, I think, more interesting than the simple foundation-superstructure metaphor suggests. In particular, swallowing "holy whoppers that an intelligent eighth grader would dismiss out of hand"[18] is not only not the core of the devotional life, it is not even an essential feature of it.

Characterizing what it is to "be religious" (to live "the life of faith," to have a "religious orientation to life") is not a simple matter. There is too much variation even among those who count as relatively clear cases of religious people or people who possess spirituality or piety. There is even a good deal of intrapersonal as well as interpersonal variation through time. Nevertheless, it seems to me that many of those in the Christian tradition who would be correctly regarded as reasonably clear and fairly normal cases of religiously oriented people possess in at least some degree characteristics like the following.

First, they have a sense of the numinous. That is, they are struck or moved, at least from time to time, by awareness of the sacred, by an apprehension of something in (or about) life or the world that is deeply mysterious, something both attractive and fearful that evokes such responses as awe and reverence, a profound solemnity, praise, contrition, and "a bowing of the head." They have, as Frederick Buechner says of Job, seen or at least glimpsed "the great glory so shot through with sheer, fierce light and life and gladness [and at least in a muffled way] heard the great voice raised in song so full of terror and wildness and beauty, that . . . all possible questions [have] melted like mist, and all possible explanations [have] withered like grass,"[19] and they have felt, at least momentarily, that "all the death that ever was, set next to life, would scarcely fill a cup."[20]

Second, they find themselves, at least from time to time, possessed of those "fruits of the spirit" that St. Paul called "love, joy [and] peace."[21] That is, they frequently, or at least occasionally, know a deep serenity, poise, tranquillity, or quietness within, a peace that is rooted in a profound sense of security despite the contingencies of life.[22] They frequently, or at least occasionally, are moved by "loving affections," feelings of tenderness and concern even for those who are full of spite, hatred, and cruelty, feelings that sometimes spill over onto nonhuman targets, and sometimes onto parts of the inanimate world.[23] And they frequently, or at least occasionally, experience (again at least in some degree) the kind of zest, enthusiasm, exhilaration, buoyancy, and energy that characterize those in the glow of first love.[24] When enjoying these conditions, such persons tend to be (relatively) free of the worries and cares that are part of the warp and woof of human existence, or if such worries and cares are present they exist, so to speak, only on the surface of their lives.[25] They tend to be free also of such negative affects as anger, envy, greed, jealousy, spite, and regret, as well as concern for the small and the petty. And they are (relatively) untouched by despair, the sense that nothing ultimately matters, as well as the kind of sadness that often afflicts those whose outlooks on life are man-centered and naturalistic.[26]

Third, more or less devoutly religious people within the Christian tradition often have certain characteristic attitudes toward life and toward some of the more fundamental events and situations in life. Thus they often regard seeking after fame, fortune, and power as wrong insofar at least as one is motivated by vanity or a desire for self-glorification. They sometimes take a similar attitude toward the pursuit of sensual pleasures (such as sexual pleasure and the delights of the palate), especially if such pursuits occupy an important place in a person's life. Attitudes of optimism, gratitude, and hope, on the other hand, are often promiment in the lives of such people. Thus, they frequently exhibit a sense of expectancy, a sense that wonderful things are in the air. They think it appropriate to look upon their lives, their health, their families and friends, their opportunities for useful work, restorative rest, and joyful play, as "gifts," "goods" relative to which we should adopt a stance at least analogous to the gratitude we feel toward those who have benefited us out of love or good will rather than by accident or because justice or minimal decency requires it. Some even adopt such an attitude toward everything that happens to them, no matter how (ostensibly) painful or destructive. Connected with this last feature is the tendency to take up, or struggle to maintain, a hopeful attitude in every situation, a sense that however bad things may appear, good can come out of them—and indeed will if one maintains the right inner condition. Such people, in other words, have a disposition that might be manifested by an insistence that life contains no irredeemably tragic situations, no situations of horror from which there is "no exit"—at least for those whose hearts are "right."[27]

Fourth, the behavior of those who live the life of faith has a characteristic shape. At least the following three behavioral features tend to be present among the devout in the Christian tradition. Such people participate in public and private "acts of worship." They regularly engage in specifically religious ceremonies or rituals, some of which are communal in character and have gained their general shape from the religious tradition in question, others of which are private in character and may or may not have a more or less reticulate form shaped by the tradition. Such people also regularly act in ways that involve putting on "the form of the servant":[28] they help those in need, take on the burdens of others, and make themselves and their re-sources—within limits—available to others. In short, their behavior exhibits the kind of orientation depicted by the picture of Christ in the Gospels, the orientation of the self-sacrificing healer of the physical and spiritual ailments of others. Last, such people act in ways designed to "share the blessing" they feel they have received through partici-pation in the life of their religious community and tradition with those who are outside "the circle of the faithful." Such acts can take many forms, but the important point is that they need not, and frequently do not, take the form of trying to get others to adopt an idiosyncratic set of metaphysics-theological beliefs.[29]

Let us say that an individual who possesses in some degree features like these is in (one form of) "the faith-state."[30] The question I want now to raise concerns the relation of the faith-state so conceived to metaphysico-theological belief.[31]

To begin, it seems apparent that having such belief is not a logically necessary condition for being in the faith-state. A person could have all the features of the sort just described and have no well-defined metaphysico-theological views whatever. In particular, he could be quite agnostic—or even atheistic—regarding the existence of God where God is conceived along anthropomorphic lines; and he could have no clear idea of what theologians who follow the mystical tradi-tion are talking about and be quite aware that this was so. Neither the absence of belief of the anthropomorphic sort nor the absence of "belief" of the mystical sort, after all, makes it impossible that one should have a sense of the numinous, be filled with peace, love and joy, hold the pursuit of worldly "success" in disdain, feel grateful for all the goods that grace one's life, participate in the religious ceremo-nies of a particular tradition, and so on.[32]

Equally obvious is the fact that possession of such metaphysico-theological belief in no way ensures that one will be in the faith-state.

Belief that a being exists who in some sense possesses such "perfections" as omniscience, omnipotence, and perfect goodness is obviously compatible with the presence of depression, consuming self-absorption, deep worries about one's fate, envy, a pervasive joy-quashing sense of guilt, pettiness, gluttony, and the absence of a sense of the numinous and of any inclination to engage in acts of public or private worship. And the same is true regarding metaphysico-theological "beliefs" of the more mystical variety, such as a "belief" that all finite things are rooted (grounded) in a reality that "transcends the subject-object structure," of which nothing can be (literally) predicated, that "breaks into" the lives of finite creatures from time to time transforming them into "saints," and so forth.

But even though metaphysico-theological belief is neither necessary nor sufficient for possession of the faith-state, it can of course co-exist with it. Moreover, it is no doubt true that, for some, such belief (or "belief") may well function to nurture and sustain many of the component-features of this state, and considerations or experiences that weaken or destroy such belief may well effectively undermine the state, too. For others, however, the conditions that nurture and sustain the faith-state and in the absence of which it withers—"FS-conditions," for short—appear not to involve metaphysico-theological beliefs at all, at least in the common understanding of what such beliefs amount to.[33]

For some of these latter people, regular participation in formal services of worship—or perhaps just bringing to mind from time to time the myths and stories of a particular tradition—are FS-conditions, in addition to being part of what the faith-state consists in. Like William James, such people find that simply clinging "to scripture-texts like 'The eternal God is my refuge,' etc., 'Come unto me, all ye that labor and are heavy-laden,' etc., 'I am the resurrection and the life' "[34] helps to keep crippling anxieties at bay even in the absence of any firm and definite metaphysico-theological convictions. D. H. Lawrence once wrote that "the miracle of the loaves and fishes is just as good to me now as when I was a child. I don't care whether it is historically a fact or not. What does it matter?"[35] For people like D. H. Lawrence, the biblical stories possess transforming power whatever their convictions about the stories' literal truth. And for such people, something like what is true of these stories also holds as regards the prayers, collects, responsive readings, hymns, sermons, and benedictions that give shape and content to worship services.

For other people, FS-conditions may obtain where only "half-

belief" in the truth of some metaphysico-theological doctrine or doc-
trinal scheme is present, where a person *half-believes* p just in case
she exhibits all (or many) of the symptoms of genuine belief that p
while in certain special circumstances but loses them as soon as the
special circumstances no longer obtain.[36] Put in a slightly different
way, FS-conditions may, for some, hold only insofar as they are able
to think of (and feel) themselves as belonging to the "world" described
by a certain theological story, in something analogous to the way in
which we often enter into the fictional worlds of novels and plays and
thereby come to feel emotions (or analogues of the emotions) that arise
in real life.[37]

And for many of those who possess to an especially high degree
various of the features defining the faith-state, the FS-conditions no
doubt involve some variant on what one might call "the monastic life":
a way of life that consists, perhaps inter alia, in physical as well as
psychological separation from the surrounding society's distractions
and temptations. The monastic life may also involve voluntary poverty,
sexual abstinence, and a strict and time-consuming regimen of public
and private prayer and meditation, and perhaps breathing exercises,
the periodic assumption of specific physical positions, manual labor of
some simple kind, and so on. (The particular shape of the monastic
life varies considerably from tradition to tradition. One possible variant
consists in participating in such a life for limited periods on a number
of different occasions.)

The fact that metaphysico-theological belief frequently plays little or
no role in what I am calling "the life of faith" goes unnoticed largely,
I suspect, because religious people almost invariably use the language
of religion when participating in public and private worship, when
giving spiritual counsel, and even in general conversation from time to
time. Thus, they pray, "Thy kingdom come, Thy will be done, on
Earth as it is in heaven"; they sing, "The one eternal God, all praised
be His name"; they remark, "the Lord hath given and the Lord hath
taken away, blessed be the name of the Lord"; they confess, "God
was in Christ reconciling the world unto Himself"; and so on. And
such linguistic acts and responses give the impression that those who
engage in them do possess metaphysico-theological convictions of a
(more or less) traditional kind, of the kind those who have taken it
upon themselves to try to interpret the liturgy and literature of their
respective traditions have typically used such language to express.

Such an impression is often not misleading, of course. But frequently
it is; frequently, those who exhibit such linguistic behavior use (and

take) the language of religion differently from the ways those for whom it expresses (more or less) traditional metaphysico-theological theories use (and take) it. The differences are more subtle than those that separate the use of 'God bless you' by the unbelieving home-owner who has just smashed his thumb with a hammer and by the traditional Lutheran pastor giving a benediction, or the use of 'It was an act of God' by a secular lawyer referring to the devastation caused by a recent hurricane and by a fundamentalist commenting on the birth of an infant with spina bifida.

Some people who live the life of faith view the religious language that pervades their worship services as analogous to the music such services involve and to the ritualistic bodily movements that often accompany the verbal acts they engage in, and hence as no more expressive of propositional content—of thoughts that are capable of truth and falsity in a straightforward sense—than this music and these bodily movements are. Such people are often not aware of having such a "view." The music is there, it plays a role in creating a certain "orientation of the soul" (so to speak), but in no way (or sense) does it *say* that such and such is the way reality is; similarly, the ritual behavior occurs, plays a similar role, and is also nonpropositional in character; and the religious language that pervades the service does not, *for them anyhow,* seem in these respects at all different from the music and the kneeling and head-bowing.

Of course, the religious language, unlike the music and the ritual behavior, often brings to mind even for these people—as suggested above—various "pictures" and stories,[38] and perhaps, depending upon their level of intellectual sophistication, various traditional metaphysico-theological doctrines as well. This fact may well play an important role in fostering and giving shape to that special "orientation of the soul" to which the music and ritual also contribute. Thus these "pictures" and stories may help catalyze various of the feelings and attitudes that enter into the faith-state as characterized above—and especially when surrounded by remarks of a kind designed specifically for that purpose and that could be made (in a slightly different form) in a linguistic context devoid of any religious vocabulary.[39] I have in mind here attitudes of hope and confidence, a feeling for the miraculous and the sacredness of life, a celebratory attitude directed toward easily neglected but nonetheless central goods of life, a renewed sense of the importance of making ourselves available to others, and so on. How this "catalyzing" operation can occur in the absence of metaphysico-theological belief might seem mysterious at first glance. But when one reflects on the powerful way (acknowledged) fiction and mental images can influence our feelings and attitudes, such effects will not be at all surprising.[40]

Then, too, these "pictures," stories and doctrines that are called to mind by the religious language in services of worship may also, for some, bring to mind a variety of religiously significant (more or less) empirical theses—garden variety "saving truths," so to speak—to which they feel at least some inclination to assent and toward which traditional theological ideas might be regarded as gesturing obliquely. The Doctrine of Creation, for example, may bring to mind the contingency of all finite (determinately characterizable) things and with it a sense of the deep mystery that anything exists at all. The Doctrine of the Fall may call to mind some of the less attractive features human beings often exhibit, along with a renewed sense of our (collective) responsibility for some of the less happy aspects of the course of history.[41] The Doctrine of Redemption may call to mind (a) the role of the life of the church in nurturing and sustaining the faith-state, together with (b) the dependence of the church's existence (and to a certain extent character) upon that extraordinary historical development that culminated in the life and ministry of Jesus of Nazareth. In particular, it may bring to mind the idea that the way of life depicted in the synoptic Gospels and variously portrayed and promulgated in the life of the church—a way of life that involves healing the sick, forgiving the fallen, refusing to judge others, being confident that all will be well for those who "lay up treasures in heaven"—leads to peace, joy, and a sense of deep blessing, whereas the only alternative is, in Santayana's phrase, a life in "the burning city of vanity," a life largely characterized by emptiness, joylessness, cynicism, and a sense of alienation.

Also, using such language in the course of worship may for people of the kind in question resemble hanging a flag from one's porch on the Fourth of July. Such linguistic acts, in other words, may symbolize such a person's sense of solidarity with a certain religious tradition and the profoundly spiritual figures who forged it, despite his inability to endorse the metaphysical views that are prominent within this tradition. Just as a certain nation may be one's own, the place that is "home" for one's soul, despite its defects (the greed and lawlessness of many of its people or the flawed character of many of its institutions); just so may a certain religious tradition be one's own, the tradition that is also "home" for one's soul—despite the superstitions of many of its adherents, the unintelligibility of many of the theological views associated with it, and the insensitivity, fanaticism, and stupidity of many of the churches and churchmen that represent it.

Finally, it should be said that it is probably characteristic of many of the faithful in whom metaphysico-theological belief resides fitfully or not at all to be open to the possibility that the theological language they employ in worship or encounter in Scripture points to truths they are presently unable to grasp or properly appreciate, but may one day see as they grow in understanding and come to possess a deeper level of spirituality.[42] Thus their relation to their religious tradition—and especially to the metaphysical ideas it contains—is often neither acceptance nor rejection; rather, in Arthur Waskow's words, they "wrestle it, fighting it and making love to it at the same time. [They] try to touch it with [their] lives."[43]

No doubt much more could be said about the detailed ways in which religious language functions in the lives of those who possess the faith-state but lack metaphysico-theological belief. But these sketchy remarks will perhaps suggest how religiosity can exist in the absence of commitment to metaphysico-theological doctrine, despite the employment by such religious types of language that frequently is used to convey a good deal of metaphysical content, and hence how it can be that the religious life can exist and even flourish without exhibiting an ostrichlike ignorance of the critical reflections that have led so many to feel that metaphysical theology of more or less traditional kinds is a dubious enterprise, at best.

Notes

1. The same is also true of the other theistically oriented traditions—the Muslim tradition in particular. See, for example, Alfred Guillaume, *Islam* (Baltimore: Penguin Books, 1954), chaps. 7 and 8 and passim; and Ninan Smart, *A Dialogue of Religions* (London: SCM Press, 1960).

2. A prominent recent exemplar of this tradition of theological thought is Paul Tillich. A few relevant passages from his *Systematic Theology* (3 volumes; Chicago: University of Chicago Press, 1951–1963) follow. "The being of God cannot be understood as the existence of a being alongside others or above others" (I, p. 235). The supranaturalistic view is the view that "separates God as a being, the highest being, from all other beings, alongside and above which he has his existence [and holds that] he has brought the universe into being at a certain moment (five thousand or five billion years ago), governs it according to a plan, directs it toward an end, interferes with its ordinary processes in order to overcome resistance and fulfil his purpose, and will bring it to

consummation in a final catastrophe. . . . Against this kind of supranaturalism the arguments of naturalism are valid" (II, p. 6). "God transcends every being and also the totality of beings—the world" (I, p. 237). God "is the ground of the structure of being. He is not subject to this structure" (I, p. 238). "The categories [time, space, causality, substance (I, p. 193), etc.] are forms of finitude" (I, p. 192). "In God as God there is no distinction between potentiality and actuality" (I, p. 242). "God . . . precedes the subject-object structure" (I, p. 172). "God can never become an object for man's knowledge or action" (I, p. 271). "God does not exist. He is . . . beyond essence and existence" (I, p. 205). "Everything religion has to say about God, including his qualities, actions, and manifestations, has a symbolic character and . . . the meaning of 'God' is completely missed if one takes the symbolic language literally" (II, p. 9).

3. Among those who conceive of God as thus only "finitely perfect" are William James and Edgar Brightman. See, for example, W. James, *The Varieties of Religious Experience* (New York: Modern Library, n.d.), Lec. XX and Postscript; and Brightman, *The Problem of God* (New York: Abingdon Press, 1930), secs. 519–29. (The phrase 'finitely perfect' is used by Cleanthes in D. Hume, *Dialogues Concerning Natural Religion* [Indianapolis: Bobbs-Merrill, 1974], part 11.)

4. See Robert Coburn, "The Hiddenness of God and Some Barmecidal God Surrogates," *Journal of Philosophy* 57 (1960).

5. See, for example, Aquinas, *Summa Contra Gentiles,* Bk. I, chaps. 5, 8, and 14 ff., and Bk. IV, chap. 1; and *Summa Theologica,* Pt. I, q. 13, parts 3 and 4, and q. 85, art. 1; and *IV Libros Sententiarum P. Lombardi,* Lib. I, dist. 22, q. 1, art. 2. (My attention was drawn to the last passage by J. Mondin, *Analogy Old and New* [Ph.D. dissertation, Harvard University, 1959], p. 240.) See also K. Barth, *Church Dogmatics,* eds. G. W. Bromiley and T. F. Torrance (Edinburgh: T. & T. Clark, 1957), Vol. 2, Pt. 1, pp. 202–29.

6. See, for example, Ninian Smart, *Reasons and Faiths* (New York: The Humanities Press, 1959), p. 44 and 44, n. 1.

7. See, for example, A. MacIntyre, "The Logical Status of Religious Belief," in S. Toulmin, R. Hepburn, and A. MacIntyre, eds., *Metaphysical Beliefs* (London: SCM Press, 1957), pp. 192 ff.

8. See, for example, Ian Crombie, "Theology and Falsification," in A. Flew and A. MacIntyre, eds., *New Essays in Philosophical Theology* (New York: The Macmillan Co., 1955), p. 122 f. and "The Possibility of Theological Statements," in B. Mitchell, ed., *Faith and Logic* (Boston: Beacon Press, 1957), p. 70 f.

9. This is the notion used by P. F. Strawson in *Individuals* (London: Methuen, 1959), pp. 226 ff.

10. See, for example, Huston Smith, *The Religions of Man* (New York: Harper & Row, 1958), p. 72.

11. Cf. Paul Tillich, *The Courage to Be* (New Haven: Yale University Press, 1952), pp. 40 ff.

12. But see also Augustine, *Confessions,* trans. R. L. Pine-Coffin (Middlesex: Penguin Book, Ltd., 1961); L. Tolstoy, *A Confession, the Gospel in Brief, and What I Believe,* trans. A. Maude (London: Oxford University Press, n.d.); W. James, *The Varieties of Religious Experience,* Lecs. VI, VII, and passim; and E. A. Burtt, ed., *The Teachings of the Compassionate Buddha* (New York: Mentor, 1955).

13. Whether the existence of a God, anthropomorphically conceived, would suffice for either task is, of course, far from clear. Bernard Williams has mounted a strong case for doubting that we can even conceive a desirable form of "endless" life after death. See his *Problems of the Self* (Cambridge: Cambridge University Press, 1973), chap. 6. And Thomas Nagel has argued with considerable force that life would remain devoid of objective meaningfulness even if such a God did exist. See *Mortal Questions* (Cambridge: Cambridge University Press, 1979), chap. 2.

14. The phrase is Wittgenstein's. See his *Tractatus Logico-Philosophicus,* trans. D. F. Pears and B. F. McGuinness (London: Routledge & Kegan Paul, 1961), p. 6.374.

15. See, for example, Robert Nozick, *Philosophical Explanations* (Cambridge: Harvard University Press, 1981), chap. 2.

16. And if Hume is right, there will be good reason for thinking that God does not exist, given the kinds and amount of contingent evil in the world. See his *Dialogues Concerning Natural Religion,* part 11. There is, it should perhaps be noted, no unanimous agreement that the traditional arguments (and their modern variants) in support of God's existence fail. But there is certainly near-unanimous agreement on this matter, at least among professional philosophers. In any case, it is undeniable that there is nothing like the kind of agreement about the cogency of these arguments that there is as regards the proofs for the soundness and completeness of first-order predicate logic or the coerciveness of the evidence for special relativity or the current view about the molecular structure of water.

17. A strong argument for a view of this kind is given by Richard Swinburne in *Faith and Reason* (Oxford: Clarendon Press, 1981), chap. 1.

18. Frederick Buechner, *Now and Then* (San Francisco: Harper & Row, 1983), p. 95.

19. Frederick Buechner, *Peculiar Treasures* (New York: Harper & Row, 1979), p. 68.

20. Buechner, *Now and Then,* p. 109.

21. Galatians 5:22 (RSV).

22. Wittgenstein captures this phenomenon in a striking way when he writes: "Religion is, as it were, the calm bottom of the sea at its deepest point, which remains calm however high the waves on the surface may be" (*Culture and Value,* trans. P. Winch [Chicago: University of Chicago Press, 1980], p. 53).

23. See, for example, William James, *The Varieties of Religious Experience,* pp. 220, 279–82. See also in this connection F. Dostoyevsky, *The Brothers*

Karamazov, trans. C. Garnett (New York: Modern Library, n.d.), Book VII, chap. 3.

24. See, for example, James, *The Varieties of Religious Experience,* pp. 221, 243, 249, 251, 388–8, 390–91, and passim.

25. See, for example, Brother Lawrence, *The Practice of the Presence of God* (Cincinnati: Forward Movement Publications, n.d.), p. 13 (top).

26. See, for example, James, *The Varieties of Religious Experience,* pp. 138 ff., 64 f., and 70.

27. See, for example, Brother Lawrence, *The Practice of the Presence of God,* p. 44 and passim; and James, *The Varieties of Religious Experience,* passim.

28. Phillipians 2:7 (RSV).

29. See H. H. Potthoff, *Acts: Then and Now* (New York: Joint Commission on Evangelism and Culture. Board of Missions of the Methodist Church, 1965), chap. 5.

30. I borrow the phrase from James, although I use it in a somewhat different way. See *The Varieties of Religious Experience,* p. 495. In different religious traditions, the faith-state can take somewhat different forms. And, of course, it can take different forms within a given tradition too. For brevity's sake, I shall hereafter omit this qualification.

31. Some may object to speaking of such a state as "the faith-state" since, as I have characterized it, a person in it may have no metaphysical beliefs that distinguish her from one who, for the most part, lacks the syndrome of features by reference to which it has been defined. Such an objection would, I think, be misplaced. In the Christian tradition, 'faith' refers to the subjective correlate of—the reception or appropriation of—revelation. Since there are nonpropositional theories of revelation, there are conceptions of faith such that faith does not consist in whole or in part in believing that certain propositions are true. See, for example, P. Tillich, *Systematic Theology,* Vol. 1, Part I, sec. 2, and Vol. 3, pp. 129 ff. and passim, and *Dynamics of Faith* (New York: Harper Torchbooks, 1957), especially chaps. 1 and 2.

32. One thinks here of Gandhi's insistence on the fragmentariness of human vision as regards theological matters and his refusal to enter into theological debate on whether God is personal or impersonal. See Margaret Chatterjee, *Gandhi's Religious Thought* (London: The Macmillan Press, 1983), especially chaps. 1 and 10.

33. There are, of course, theories of the nature of religious belief according to which being in the faith-state—or something very similar—is what such belief amounts to. See, for example, R. B. Braithwaite, "An Empiricist's View of the Nature of Religious Belief," in J. Hick, ed., *The Existence of God* (New York: The Macmillan Co., 1964); Wittgenstein, *Culture and Value,* p. 64 and passim; and R. Coburn, "Animadversions on a Wittgensteinian Apologetic," *Perkins Journal* 24 (1971).

34. James, *The Varieties of Religious Experience,* p. 158. The account from which the passage comes is autobiographical.

35. Quoted in Frank Cioffi, "Wittgenstein and the Fire-Festival," in I. Block, ed., *Perspectives on the Philosophy of Wittgenstein* (Oxford: Basil Blackwell, 1981), p. 227.

36. The notion of "half-belief" is due to H. H. Price. See his *Belief* (London: George Allen & Unwin, 1969), Ser. II, Lec. 4, and "Half-Belief," *Proceedings of the Aristotelian Society,* Suppl. vol. 38 (1964).

37. Cf. Kendall Walton, "Fearing Fictions," *Journal of Philosophy,* 75 (1978), esp. secs. III–VII. Cf. also Coburn, "The Hiddenness of God and Some Barmecidal God Surrogates," 705 ff.

38. Preeminently (1) the "picture" of the world as a (kind of) screen behind which dwells "the eternal" (cf. N. Smart, *Reasons and Faiths,* p. 44 f.) or of the spatiotemporal order as existing on a plane that is embedded in a three-dimensional space from which "revelatory" intrusions periodically come (cf. Tillich, *Systematic Theology,* passim); and (2) "stories" about the first man and woman in the garden, a people's entering into a covenant with a supernatural being, a whale swallowing a prophet, Abraham ("the father of a multitude") readying his son for sacrifice as a demonstration of his faith, God ("the father of all mankind") sacrificing his son to save mankind, etc.

39. Remarks like the following that appear in typical pastoral prayers are cases in point: (a) "And grant that our hearts may be filled with gratitude for the love of friends and family that nourish us, for the wise counsellors whose words have lighted our paths, for the men and women of stature, living and dead, in fellowship with whom we discover our true selves." (b) "And quicken and renew our sense of the importance of our own lives and the deep significance of the many opportunities that fill our days for small acts of kindness and forgiveness and healing."

40. See in this connection Walton, "Fearing Fictions"; and Jerome Singer, *Imaging and Daydream Methods in Psychotherapy and Behavior Modification* (New York: Academic Press, 1974); and Jerome Singer and Kenneth Pope, eds., *The Power of Human Imagination: New Methods in Psychotherapy* (New York: Plenum Press, 1978).

41. It may even bring to mind various of the ideas Herbert Morris has assembled in his rich and suggestive attempt to uncover the truth(s) in the idea presented in *The Brothers Karamazov* that "we all are responsible for everything." See his paper "Shared Guilt," in *On Guilt and Innocence* (Berkeley: University of California Press, 1976).

42. They may, for example, have an inclination to think along lines of the kind Wittgenstein adumbrated in the following remark: "In religion every level of devoutness must have its appropriate form of expression which has no sense at a lower level. This doctrine, which means something at a higher level, is null and void for someone who is still at the lower level; we *can* only understand it *wrongly* and so these words are *not* valid for such a person" (*Culture and Value,* p. 32).

43. Arthur Waskow, *Godwrestling* (New York: Schocken Books, 1978), p. 11.

CHAPTER EIGHT

Truth, Epistemological Optimism, and the Limits of Science

I

The notion that some statements about, for example, past wars, the eruptions of volcanoes, the future of mankind, and the sequence of prime numbers are true and others false is one we can hardly imagine trying to do without. Moreover, central to the idea that many people prereflectively operate with is the thought that what makes a statement true when it is true is its "agreement with reality" or its "fitting the facts," where the structure of reality or the shape of the facts is conceived to be quite independent of the mental apparatus or processes of any knower or group of knowers. In other words, it is commonly taken as obvious that not only can our beliefs and judgments about the world around us be correct or in error, but also that the way the world is does not depend upon believers—their existence, their constitutions, their intellectual activities, their conceptual repertoires, or what have you.[1] Gravitation operates as it does and the laws of electromagnetism are as they are whatever may be true about the existence or natures of any cognitive agents. And the same is true as regards the number of twin primes, the origin of life, and the molecular structure of water. At any rate, so many people prereflectively think.

It is also part and parcel of the ordinary conception of truth that the truth about reality is both consistent and fully determinate. It is consistent in the sense that there is no proposition about any phenomenon or aspect of reality—indeed no proposition whatever—such that both it and its negation are true. Convince the man in the street that the Democrats will control the U.S. Senate in 1992 and you will *eo ipso* have convinced him that it is false that the Democrats will not control the Senate in 1992—and similarly for any other proposition. The truth about the world, furthermore, is ordinarily thought fully determinate in the sense that, for any proposition whatever about any aspect of reality, or about reality as a whole, either it or its negation is true.[2] Thus, ordinary people prereflectively take it for granted that either Caesar had an egg for breakfast on his third birthdy or it is not the case that he had an egg for breakfast on this third birthday; that either there are an infinite number of twin primes or there are not; that either the next president of the United States will die by an assassin's bullet or it is not the case . . . , and so on. In short, central to the ordinary conception of truth is the idea of a body or system of propositions such that were anyone to know the truth of the entire collection, no doubt *per impossibile,* it would not only follow that there would be no facts concerning reality of which he or she was ignorant, but also (a) that there would be some propositions that would not logically follow from those known[3] and (b) that one of every pair of contradictory propositions would be among those known.[4]

Closely associated with the foregoing ideas are two others. Although they are not as fundamental as the former ideas, they are also quite pervasive in our intellectual culture, at least among the reasonably well educated. The first might be called "the thesis of epistemological optimism." It consists in the thought that if we human beings are sufficiently diligent and sufficiently careful in our search for truth, we will—in the absence of natural or other catastrophe—continually expand and deepen our knowledge of the world and our place in it, and thus gradually come closer and closer to realizing the ideal of omniscience. The second of these further ideas might be labeled "the thesis of the sovereignty of science." It is the thesis that the only genuine knowledge is scientific knowledge—the knowledge that falls under the headings "mathematics" and "empirical science"—and, accordingly, that the only procedures that are reliable for the purpose of expanding and deepening our knowledge are those associated with mathematics and the empirical sciences: the formal methods of mathematics and the experimental, statistical, and hypothetico-deductive methods of the empirical sciences.

These ideas too are not unproblematic. In what follows, I shall indicate some of the considerations that make clear why and in what sense this is so.

II

Let us call the view that the truth about reality is "consistent," "fully determinate," and "mind-independent" in the senses indicated above "the realist theory of truth," or more briefly, "realism." It seems clear upon reflection that realism, so understood, will be false if the following conditions are met: (1) a theory about some aspect of the world that would be justified under ideal epistemic conditions could be false only on pain of contradiction; and (2) what it is to be "justified under ideal epistemic conditions" as regards this or that category or propositions[5] is determined by or dependent upon some contingent aspect of our natures, that is, some facts about us that could have been otherwise, such as the structure of our potential conceptual repertoire, or our intuitive sense of simplicity and elegance, or the weights we give in deciding the degree of confirmation that follows upon a scientific theory's "robustness."[6] For under these conditions, the truth about reality, or the way the world is, will depend upon contingent facts about us. It is quite plausible to think that condition (2) does in fact hold. Thus it is plausible, for example, to suppose that there are limits to our capacity to form concepts; and it could not fail to be the case that what concepts it is possible for us to acquire is a contingent fact about us.[7] It is also plausible to think that our intuitive sense of simplicity and elegance and what metaphysical propositions strike us as self-evident depend upon the facts about our constitutions that could have been otherwise. Hence, it seems that realism can be true only if condition (1) fails.

So if (1) and (2), then realism is false. But (2) is quite plausible. Hence, if the realist theory of truth holds, (1) is very likely false. But this means that if realism holds, then plausibly all the members of any consistent set of beliefs we have about the (extra-mental) world could be false.[8] After all, if a theory that would be justified under ideal epistemic conditions could be false, then surely any theory or belief about the (extra-mental) world we might have could be false. But if any theory or belief of ours could be false, surely any collection of such beliefs might all be false, as long as the collection was free of contradictory beliefs.

The view that such radical error is logically possible is difficult to accept. In the first place, if this view were correct, it is difficult to see how we could possess justifiable confidence that either our ordinary commonsense beliefs or our scientific beliefs about the world come anywhere near the truth. The fact that scientific theories have been steadily displaced by others that are more powerful engines of explanation and prediction would not provide any basis for confidence. For if radical error of the kind in question is possible, how could it not be the case that all these theories might be equally far from the truth? Indeed, the epistemic standards that govern such theory replacement might be leading us astray in a systematic way.

Here is one way of developing this connection of realism with skepticism. If our beliefs about the world could (in the relevant sense, see n. 8) be largely false, then it's possible that two groups of inquirers should exist, G and G*, who are in "epistemic equilibrium" as regards the fundamental features of the world, but whose overall views about these features are nonetheless mutually contradictory. Here I understand the idea of epistemic equilibrium as follows. Someone's view about some feature or aspect of the world is in epistemic equilibrium provided that he or she has taken into account everything that is relevant in deciding what view to accept, has good reason for thinking this is so, and has in consequence settled upon such and such a stand on the matter at issue. Alternatively, to be in epistemic equilibrium regarding some aspect or feature of reality is to have developed a view as regards the question at issue after having undergone an epistemically ideal process of inquiry vis-à-vis this question. And the reason the views of two such groups could conflict derives from the plausibility of (2) above (see the first paragraph of this section). Put in a nutshell, the criteria of intelligibility, on the basis of which certain views are ruled out, that seem natural to the G-thinkers, could be very different from those that appeal to the G*-thinkers.[9] But if this kind of situation is possible, then it's also possible that these groups should come into contact with each other and discover both their disagreement and the epistemological position each group occupies with respect to its convictions about the fundamental features of the world. Such a state of affairs could not but undermine the rational confidence each group places in its belief-system. For since *ex hypothesi* each group had already taken account of everything relevant in deciding what to believe in the area in question and had good reason for thinking this was so, each would have reason to believe that its beliefs about the fundamental features of reality might well be false and that nothing it could learn or discover by reflection would show whether this was so. But if the truth of realism makes a situation of this kind possible, then it follows that *our* grounds for *our* fundamental beliefs are suspect as well. After all, if inquirers in epistemic equilibrium as regards the fundamental features of the world could, under easily conceivable circumstances, come to see that the grounds for their beliefs are suspect, surely our actual epistemic situation can hardly be any better.

To put the problem in a somewhat different way, if any collection of our ordinary and scientific beliefs that constitute a consistent set could (in the relevant sense; see n. 8) all be mistaken, then it is hard to understand how we could possibly certify them apart from some access to reality that is not mediated by them. But the idea of our grasping reality as it is, independent of our methods of representing it, on the face of it lacks clear sense. To make a judgment about the world is, after all, to make use of some method of conceptually representing it. And what would it be to grasp reality as it is without making any judgments about it? Thus it would seem that on the view in question the world, and *a fortiori* the truth about it, is ineluctably hidden—hidden, as it is sometimes put, behind an impenetrable "veil of representations."

Second, and worse, the view that our ordinary picture of the world could (in the nonepistemic sense; see note 8) be radically mistaken entails that we could (in the relevant sense) be mistaken in thinking (a) that the people we know and love are not really impostors, owing for example to an invasion of "body snatchers" last spring, (b) that the trees and rocks, houses and cars which are thought to surround us in daily life continue to exist when no one is observing them, (c) that our experiences to date are not wholly the result of brain probes engineered by diabolical superscientists of whose existence we have not a clue, (d) that the world did not come into existence two minutes ago, complete with all the memories and other (deceptive) evidences of a long history reaching back to the (apparent) big bang, and even (e) that there exists—or has ever existed—anything other than the mental states of which we are now currently aware. The central difficulty to which these "possibilities" gives rise is not just that we cannot take them seriously, although that is certainly true. Nor is it the related difficulty that nothing could *reasonably* be taken as evidence that any of these possibilities obtains. (As Wittgenstein remarks, "What could make me doubt whether this person here is N.N., whom I have known for years? Here a doubt would seem to drag everything with it and plunge it into chaos."[10] That is to say, presented with ostensible evidence that some fundamental part of my picture of the world is false, "the foundation of all judging would be taken away from me."[11] It is just *"unthinkable* that I should stay in the saddle however much the facts bucked."[12]) Rather, the central problem is that—at least in the case of the last three—a plausible case can be made for thinking that these alleged "possibilities" are bogus, and this for reasons quite independent of their apparent immunity to proof.

Consider, for example, the ostensible possibility that the world came into existence two minutes ago just as it then was—excluding, of course, all the "facts" that make true various descriptions of it that entail the existence of things prior to two minutes ago. If this were in fact the case, then the words we employ in constructing a sentence like 'The world came into existence two minutes ago' (S) have no established usage.[13] But except in special cases where a word, or use of a word, is introduced into a language by stipulation, a word's meaning is a function of the way it has been used in the past.[14] Except perhaps in special cases like the above, one uses a word correctly when and only when one's use conforms to the way it is commonly employed in one's linguistic community. But if this is right, it follows that if the world did in fact come into existence two minutes ago, S would be devoid of sense; its component words would not be the words of an established natural language; the idea that these words were being used correctly would fail of application. But this means that the state of affairs in question is expressible only if it fails to obtain. But if it cannot be expressed if true, could it be believed or could the possibility of its being true even be entertained? Not, it seems, if thoughts of this sort are language-dependent, as again seems at least plausible; that is, not if thoughts of this sort are capable of being entertained only by beings who have the linguistic capacities and resources to express them. But if this is right, the view that all (or most of) our beliefs about (extramental) reality might (in the relevant sense) be mistaken cannot be correct, since we surely can entertain the proposition that the world came into existence two minutes ago. In any case, any view that, together with other obvious truths, implies that we might be wrong in thinking that we can entertain such propositions, is one we can embrace only if the alternatives are even less palatable.

There is still another problem to which the idea that our currently accepted picture of the world might (in the relevant sense) be radically mistaken leads. If such radical error is possible, then it would seem possible that there should be a plurality of radically opposed "theories of the world" or "ways of conceptualizing reality," most of which misrepresent the way things really are, in some cases in very fundamental respects. But it is hard to accept this picture of a multiplicity of possible, but radically different, representational schemes standing over against a world which matches one and not the rest. This is so because of the difficulty of making sense of the idea of there being radically alternative ways of thinking about the world. To understand this difficulty, ask yourself what would show that some group of aliens from another planet both (a) had the intellectual equipment necessary to possess highly articulate, reasoned views about the nature of reality, and yet (b) did *not* operate with the fundamental scheme of concepts that lies behind and informs our own thinking at every level, or did not come to believe any of the things we believe when placed in similar perceptual situations. (By "the fundamental scheme of concepts" in question, I mean, the scheme that includes such notions as *space* and *matter, past* and *future, things* and *properties, concrete* and *abstract, truth* and *fact, necessity* and *possibility, objective* and *subjective, cause* and *effect, event* and *state of affairs*). Such evidence would have to give us reason to think, for example, that they do come to have (what they regard as) well-founded beliefs when their sense organs are affected by, say, the electromagnetic radiation reflected from the surfaces of the objects in their vicinity (as we would put it), but nonetheless *not* give us reason to think they come to have beliefs at all like the ones we would develop in the same circumstances. It is difficult enough for us to feel confident that we understand the views of tribes like the Azande with their notions of magic, witchcraft, and oracles.[15] And these people share almost all of the general nonscientific beliefs about the world that we develop in the first few years of life. Were the conceptual and theoretical differences even greater, it is not difficult to feel that our capacities to understand would quickly reach their limits.[16]

III

On the basis of considerations like the above, the ordinary way of thinking about truth can seem less than fully satisfactory. But when one reflects on what appear to be the most plausible alternative conceptions, the possibility of discovering an importantly different but, all things considered, more satisfactory view seems quite hopeless.

The difficulties the realist view encounters all spring from the fact that it appears inexorably to lead to a logical gulf between the conditions that justify a view and the conditions that make it true. For it is this gulf between justification-conditions and truth-conditions, according to realism, that issues in the apparent inaccessibility of the truth, the list of ostensibly unthinkable possibilities, and the plurality of possible, but radically different, representational schemes. To develop a plausible alternative conception, it would appear necessary to bridge this gulf, and this is in fact exactly what the major contenders do.

According to the least sophisticated of these, a theory's truth simply consists in its being acceptable by current lights. In other words, on this conception the truth is identified with the going views, whatever they may happen to be, provided they are in some sense warranted. (What shape the warrant takes will, of course, vary with the kind of view or proposition in question.) I shall hereafter call this the theory of *Truth as Rational Acceptability*.[17]

The difficulties with a theory like this are, of course, both legion and obvious. First, it entails that Ptolemaic astronomy was once true but is no longer. But this conflicts with the firm intuition that the truth about such things as the structure of the solar system is not thus relative to different temporal eras or changeable with changing evidence. Second, the conception implies, in an area where several incompatible theories have equal warrant (as was the case a few years ago with the steady state and the big bang cosmological theories) either that both are true or perhaps that there simply is no truth in the area in question. But this consequence flies in the face of firm intuitions concerning truth's consistency and determinateness, intuitions that, as we have seen, underlie the ordinary conception. Third, the theory seems to be implicitly circular. What, after all, is it for a proposition to be "acceptable by current lights"? Presumably, it's for it to be beliefworthy. But to be worthy of being believed is no different from being worthy of being believed *true*.

Finally, when we apply the theory to itself by asking what it is, according to this theory of truth, for *it* to be true, we get a very unhappy consequence. Let us call "T" the theory that for a proposition to be true is just for it to be acceptable by current lights. Then what it is for T to be true is just for T to be acceptable by current lights. So (a) if T, then T will be false if at some time in the future, some other theory of truth has better epistemic credentials. But (b) we do not know that that won't happen. So (c) we do not know that T won't be false next week. But (d) if we do not know that T won't be false next week, surely we do not have adequate reason for accepting T now. But (e) if we do not have adequate reason now for accepting T, then T is false—given anyhow that T is either true or false.

Once the way of connecting justification-conditions with truth-conditions that the theory of Truth as Rational Acceptability involves is seen to be inadequate, the obvious way to go seems to be to identify truth with "ideal rational acceptability," that is, with justifiability under ideal epistemic conditions.[18] For then one is forced to hold, counterintuitively, neither that outmoded views were once true, nor that our current views could not fall short of the truth. Also, in the case of two conflicting views with equal warrant, one is not compelled to hold either the idea that contradictory theories might both be true or the idea that there is no truth in the domain they cover. And last, such a view clearly does not entail that it will be false provided a different view comes to have better epistemic credentials at some time in the future.

Unfortunately, upon reflection we find that this *prima facie* more attractive conception—hereafter called *Truth as Ideal Rational Acceptability* or "TIRA" for short—fares no better than its predecessor. To begin, such a view is obviously not at all plausible when "ideal epistemic conditions" include conditions anyone takes to be epistemically ideal and when a belief is held to be justifiable in certain conditions whenever anyone holds it to be justifiable under those conditions. Many "born again" Christians, after all, think that we are justified in believing that a man called Jonah lived for a while in the stomach of a whale, presumably owing to a certain implicit conception of "ideal epistemic conditions" and what beliefs are justifiable under the conditions taken to be epistemically ideal. But few will be happy with a theory of truth that turns the Jonah story into historical truth, given the existence of people with ideas like these. Once this obvious point is made, it is not difficult to see how the theory should be developed. The most attractive version is the one that explicates the notion of "ideal epistemic conditions" and the idea of beliefs being justified under certain circumstances by reference to the conceptions that would be accepted in a state of "reflective equilibrium" vis-à-vis the notions in question, that is, the conceptions that would be settled upon once all possible arguments for and against all possible such conceptions had been considered and carefully evaluated.[19] Construing the theory in question in this way clearly circumvents difficulties that arise owing to subjective or ill-considered ideas about what it is to be in ideal epistemic conditions or what it is for a belief to be justifiable under certain circumstances.

Once this clarification of the view is at hand, however, we see immediately that its evaluation calls for consideration of two cases. First is the case in which there is, as a matter of necessity, agreement about (a) what would count as "ideal epistemic conditions" for the different categories of proposition, as well as agreement about (b) when a proposition would be "justified" under various conditions in the sense that rational agents in any possible world would concur on these matters once they had achieved reflective equilibrium regarding them.[20] And second is the case where such agreement would not be forthcoming even in reflective equilibrium.

One difficulty should the first case obtain is that then TIRA contains no guarantee that it will never turn out that two incompatible theories about some subject-matter are equally justifiable under ideal epistemic conditions, or even that under such conditions no theory as regards some class of phenomena will turn out to be clearly justifiable. Hence, the view can obviously be faulted for flouting the strong intuitions behind the consistency and determinateness requirements that undergird the realist view. A theory clearly won't do, in other words, if it allows the possibility, for all we can see, that contradictory theories should both be true or that nothing should be true as regards some phenomenon or range of phenomena.

On the other hand, if the second case holds (that rational agents disagree, even in reflective equilibrium, on what count as ideal epistemic conditions for the different categories of proposition, as well as on what it is for a proposition to be justified in various circumstances), then TIRA entails that no propositions will be true (or false) *tout court,* but only relative to some conception of ideal epistemic conditions and some conception of justification—conceptions that could well have been otherwise. This implies, however, that there just is no way the world is independent of the idiosyncratic modes of representation of given groups of inquirers, an idea that on the face of it is quite difficult to credit.

Furthermore, if we ask what it is that makes a proposition like *There is a brown table in the corner of the room* ("B" say) true, the answer, if the second case obtains, will have to be something like this: that the world *an sich* (i.e., the world as it is independently of being represented in one way or another) has the power of causing beings with constitutions like ours to represent it as containing a room with a brown table in one of its corners (call this proposition "P").[21] But if this is right, two questions immediately arise. First, how are we to understand the truth-conditions of propositions like P? They can hardly take the form of the truth-conditions of propositions like B. Second, how are we to understand the expression 'beings with constitutions like ours' that is used in expressing P? It cannot refer to persons as conceived in our current theory of the world. For that theory is supposed to be a function of our contingent constitutions and thus cannot be appealed to in formulating propositions like P that presumably hold independent of the particular representational schemes of any finite group of inquirers. P will have to be construed as making reference to "noumenal" inquirers who have such and such constitutions. But then the use of the plural in 'inquirers' becomes problematic and the correctness of P accordingly doubtful.

There is a further difficulty if the second case holds. Suppose we accept the view that what we understand when we understand what a given proposition asserts is what would have to be the case for the proposition to be true. (The view that what we understand when we understand propositon p is given by the conditions under which we are, or would be, justified in asserting p is, after all, quite counterintuitive. For it implies that [more or less orthodox] Christians and Muslims do not hold contradictory theological views, assuming that the justification-conditions of each theological position involve essential reference to their respective scriptural foundations.) Suppose further that two groups of inquirers—A and B—exist who would arrive at different conceptions of justification and ideal epistemic conditions (for different categories of proposition) were they to achieve reflective equilibrium as regards these notions. Finally, suppose that the members of A and the members of B ostensibly agree on the truth of some sentence, such as 'Zinc dissolves in H_2SO_4' (S). Then they will not accept the same proposition in virtue of believing S, if TIRA is sound, and this even if all the evidence indicates that they mean the same thing by all the expressions that appear in S and even if they have exactly the same physico-chemical theories. For the truth-condition of the propositon S expresses for A will be different from the truth-condition of the proposition S expresses for B. (The truth-condition of the proposition S expresses for A will be that S is justifiable in conditions C; whereas the truth-condition of the proposition S expresses for B will be that S is, say, justifiable* in conditions C*.) But this consequence of the suppositions indicated is absurd. So TIRA must be false, if the second case mentioned above holds.

It would seem, then, that TIRA crries high costs whether there would or would not be agreement in reflective equilibrium about the notions of ideal epistemic conditions and the justifiability of claims under various circumstances. But the problems for this view are even more serious than I have so far indicated. For it faces three more difficulties, whichever of the two cases I have distinguished obtains.

First is the difficulty, already mentioned in connection with the view of Truth as Rational Acceptability, that the account suffers from circularity inasmuch as there is no distinction between accepting a proposition and accepting it as true. Closely related to this difficulty is a second, that it is hard to see what arguments would possibly support holding that the best conception of ideal epistemic conditions (relatively to some category of propositions) and the best conception of being justifiably accepted under certain circumstances, are such and such once one rules out appeal to the idea that operating with one such set of conceptions rather than another is more likely to lead to *true* beliefs. Yet this appeal has to be ruled out if the idea of truth is not to be implicitly involved in the analysans of the view of Truth as Ideal Rational Acceptability.

Finally, there is the following very serious problem for the theory of Truth as Ideal Rational Acceptability if what it amounts to can be expressed thus: a proposition p is true iff if there is (or were) an ideally rational inquirer in ideal epistemic conditions, then he or she accepts (or would accept) p.[22] I shall call this version of TIRA "A." Let "B" be the statement "If there is an ideally rational inquirer in ideal epistemic conditions, then he or she accepts C," and "C" be the statement that there is an ideally rational inquirer in ideal epistemic conditions. With these labels to hand, the problem in question can be framed thus. It is plausible to think that B is true. After all, wouldn't an ideally rational inquirer in ideal epistemic conditions be aware that he or she is ideally rational and that he or she is in ideal epistemic conditions? Indeed, it seems that one could reasonably build such awareness into the account of what it is to be in ideal epistemic conditions. But if B is true and A is the correct view as regards the nature of truth, then C could not fail to be true. For A clearly entails that C is true iff if there is (or were) an ideally rational inquirer in ideal epistemic conditions, then he or she accepts (or would accept) C. And if what follows the 'iff' is true given B, and the biconditional holds given A, clearly C is entailed by A and B. But no one wants a theory of truth that, when taken together with a proposition it is difficult to deny, requires that there exists an ideally rational inquirer in ideal epistemic conditions—at any rate, if, as again seems plausible, one is in epistemically ideal conditions only if all possible support that might conceivably bear upon the justifiability of any proposition one might wish to mention is available to one.[23]

IV

In view of the foregoing discussion, many of our prereflective convictions do not appear to yield a coherent view as regards the nature of truth. Our convictions about the consistency, determinateness, and mind-independence of truth, together with convictions that make us doubtful that truth is relative to historical epochs or conceptions of justifiability and the like, the firm belief that it is at least an open question whether there exist any ideally rational inquirers who are in ideal epistemic conditions, and so on, incline us strongly toward a realist view and away from all views that indissolubly link the truth of propositions with our actual or potential warrant for asserting these propositions. On the other hand, convictions concerning the epistemic status of firmly entrenched commonsense and scientific beliefs, the implausibility of the idea that our best methods for learning about the world might be systematically leading us astray, the truth of the thesis that we can entertain such propositions as that the world came into existence two minutes ago, and the idea that the meanings of our words are connected with the ways these words are regularly used by speakers of the language in which they occur, attract us away from realism and toward the general kind of view that is sometimes called "anti-realist."

Nonetheless, because of the number and seriousness of the difficulties to which views of the latter kind appear liable, I suspect the best solution to the general problem this discussion raises will involve rejecting all conceptions of this sort in favor of some variant of realism. But I am also reasonably confident that no such view will be without significant costs. Many things that strike us prereflectively as obvious will have to be given up or seriously qualified. Here, too, the optimal view—the best view all things considered—will fall far short of what we might hope for.

V

The thesis of epistemological optimism and the thesis of the sovereignty of science are just as problematic as the notion of truth. I shall conclude the present chapter by noting a few considerations that make clear why this is so.

The thesis of epistemological optimism, it will be recalled, is the thesis that sufficiently diligent and sufficiently careful inquiry will, if prolonged indefinitely, bring us closer and closer to realizing the ideal of omniscience. It is the thesis, in other words, that we cannot help but expand and deepen our knowledge if we keep struggling to do so with the kind of motivation and rationality that has characterized our most impressive cognitive achievements in the last few thousand years. Despite the plausibility this thesis may have at first glance, its truth is in fact not at all obvious. To see why, it is sufficient to imagine some possible lines of development that would have the effect of derailing our search for truth and, further, do so in ways that do not undercut either our motivation, our rationality, our technological resources, or our existence.

A somewhat fanciful possibility of the kind in question is this. Suppose we were to come by (apparently) decisive evidence to support the view (a) that our conscious mental life depends upon what goes on in our brains in the sense that for every mental state (or event) there is a condition of (or occurrence in) the owner's brain that is causally sufficient for his or her being in that state (or undergoing that event), and (b) that a group of intelligent aliens somewhere in the galaxy are now and have always been affecting what happens in our brains in such a way as to determine every aspect of our mental lives throughout our lives. Such evidence might take the form of discoveries about their existence, their technological capabilities, and their current and past intentions with regard to us. The reason such evidence would derail us is, of course, not far to seek. To accept the view it supports would undercut both its own value as evidence and all other evidence for conclusions about the nature of the world. For to the extent we had reason to think (a) and (b) both true, to that same extent we would have reason to think that our ostensible observations were worthless as evidence of anything. So decisive evidence that (a) and (b) are true would be decisive evidence that we lacked evidence for any facts about the world. In short, it appears at least logically possible that the world be such that the possibility of developing a view that adequately takes account of all the ostensible evidence we gather is logically impossible.

Two possibly more realistic stories that might one day be confirmed and that would have similar effects on our epistemological pursuits are the following. First, suppose that evidence were to become increasingly impressive in support of the view that the potential conceptual repertoire[24] of human beings, that is, the system of concepts it is possible for human beings to acquire, is genetically based in the way or sense in which eye color, skin pigmentation, and blood type are, by current lights, genetically based. Then we would be in the epistemologically untoward position of being compelled by the evidence to believe that the thesis of epistemological optimism was probably false, since the likelihood that the correct laws of nature, for example, could be formulated by the use of concepts it was possible for us to acquire would be, on the face of it, no greater than the likelihood, say, that the noumenal world of Kant possessed spatiotemporal structure. In other words, it would be the sheerest coincidence if the concepts in our potential conceptual repertoire should turn out to be adequate for stating such fundamental truths about the world—given anyhow, what seems plausible (and might well be discovered), that the nature of our potential conceptual repertoire is not to be explained by reference to the selective advantage of having genes that express themselves phe-notypically in the possession of a repertoire that contains concepts adequate for formulating the fundamental laws of nature.

The second story is similar. Suppose the evidence becomes increas-ingly powerful that the correct explanation of the existence of the intellectual capacities of human beings that underlie our greatest achievements in mathematics and physics is that these capacities derive from the presence in the human gene pool of genes of a kind that conferred a selective advantage upon our remote ancestors via other phenotypic expressions of these genes. In other words, suppose that the correct explanation of the existence of these capacities turns out to be, at bottom, a reflection of the phenomenon of pleiotropy. Then we would lose rational confidence that the exercise of these capacities is bringing us steadily closer to the truth about the basic structure of the physical world. For it does seem clear that we could have evolved with capacities that led us to develop very different kinds of theories. We might, for example, have been constituted so as to make use of positional rather than nonpositional concepts—the con-cept *grue* rather than the concept *green,* for example, where x is *grue* $=_{df} x$ is examined before A.D. 2000 and is green; otherwise x is blue— and similarly for a whole range of notions. (See also in this connection the last paragraph of section II above and n. 9.) But if this is right and it is also the case that the correct explanation of the existence of these capacities is of the sort indicated, then it would be the sheerest accident if the exercise of the intellectual capacities in question did lead to the truth, since it would not have been their truth-yielding features that conferred a selective advantage on those of our ancestors who possessed the genes that expressed themselves phenotypically in the existence of these capacities.

In sum, then, it seems that although the thesis of epistemological optimism might be true, its truth is not obvious since—perhaps *inter alia*—we might find, as inquiry proceeds, either that we cannot con-struct a picture of the world that enables us to do justice to the evidence we possess without undermining its own credibility, or that the probability is vanishingly small that we possess the intellectual resources necessary for discovering fundamental truths.

Moreover, the thesis of the sovereignty of science (the thesis according to which all genuine knowledge is scientific knowledge and the only reliable procedures for expanding and deepening our knowledge are those associated with the empirical sciences and mathematics) is perhaps in even a worse position than that of the foregoing thesis. For though the latter might well be true for all we currently know, the former has every appearance of being false, despite the stupendous and even awesome achievements in disciplines like mathematics and physics that apparently make the doctrine attractive to those to whom it appeals.

To see that this is so, it is not necessary to show, as has often been attempted, that (a) the very activities of evidence-gathering or theorizing of the kinds characteristic of the most impressive scientific achievements would not be possible unless there was a lot that human beings know (or are capable of knowing) independent of such activities. (Recall, for example, the arguments of Descartes, Kant and, more recently, Strawson.) Nor is it required to establish that (b) there are aspects of reality that cannot be apprehended by the pursuit of deeper and more comprehensive, well-confirmed scientific theories, aspects that can be grasped in ways that are significantly different from the ways of getting at the world which the use of scientific methodologies involve. (Recall, for example, orthodox Christian apologetics, Leibnizian rationalism, the early Russell on universals, and the long history of mysticism spanning both East and West.) Although many of these lines of thought are far from persuasive, it is not obvious that all arguments of these general kinds fail. I am not convinced, for example, that the materials for a forceful argument in support of transcendental knowledge of the sort that arguments for (a) seek to establish have not been provided by Wittgenstein in *On Certainty*. And Thomas Nagel's case for the existence of facts that elude the sort of "objective" approach to the world that characterizes the empirical sciences makes the truth of (b) at least plausible.[25]

But however this may be, it suffices, I suggest, to show the falsity of the thesis of the sovereignty of science merely to call to mind questions like the following:

(1) What is it for a fact (or collection of facts) to be evidence for the truth of some theory or conjecture?
(2) Is belief in the truth of a well-confirmed theory that has impli-

cations that transcend the limits of experience irrational? Or, if not irrational, does such belief go beyond what rationality requires?

(3) Is the fact that S is true the same fact as the fact that S?

(4) What is being said when it is said, for example, that Lincoln's assassination is continually receding further and further into the past, or that Christmas 1999 is steadily getting closer to the present? And does the truth of such remarks entail the existence of facts that cannot be expressed without the use of temporal indexicals—expressions like 'present', 'now', 'five days ago', and so on?

(5) Are there causal relations that hold between substances (or agents) and events or states of affairs, causal relations that cannot be "reduced" to (or analyzed by reference to) the kind of causal relations that hold between events or states of affairs?

(6) When we believe, for example, that we could have been shorter or heavier on our twentieth birthdays than we actually were, do we *ipso facto* hold that among the things that really exist are "nonactual possible worlds"? If so, how should we conceive of these "entities"? Should we, for example, think of them as collections of abstract entities (e.g., states of affairs) that are part of the actual world? Or should we think of them as made up of concrete objects (like you and me) that happen to be causally and spatiotemporally isolated from any objects that exist in the actual world?

(7) Might the best possible life for one person differ in character from the best possible life for another person, even though both are in exactly the same circumstances?

(8) Is it possible to know that memory is generally reliable without presupposing the general reliability of memory?

(9) Are moral judgments like "Abortion is morally impermissible except when it is necessary to save the life of the mother" and "It is not in general morally required to come to the aid of another who is in need or jeopardy when doing so carries a substantial risk to life or limb for the agent or someone he especially cares about" properly thought of as true or false? And if so, in what does their truth or falsity consist? Are there, for example, irreducible moral facts the existence of which is independent of the beliefs or attitudes of any and all rational agents that happen to exist? Is the truth of such a judgment a matter of its being the case that it would be assented to by any

rational agent (or, alternatively, any human being) who has gone through a certain kind of intellectual process—perhaps *per impossibile?*

(10) What are the truth conditions for statements of the form "Person *a*, who exists now, is the very same person as *b*, who existed two weeks ago?"

The reason that questions like these bear upon the thesis of the sovereignty of science is, to begin with, that they are not questions of a sort that can be answered by engaging in investigations of the kinds characteristic of the empirical sciences like physics or by the use of mathematical methods. This fact, of course, does not suffice by itself to topple the thesis in question. It also has to be made out that such questions have knowable answers, that there are truths to be discovered in the areas they define. This is admittedly more difficult. But at least this should be clear: virtually no one who understands what is at issue here doubts that at least some questions of the general kind to which these belong have answers. Moreover, given the extraordinary inventiveness of human beings and the ingenuity of the reflection such questions have so far elicited, it seems that anyone who maintains that there are no answers to such questions or that we can never know the answers to them must surely bear the burden of proof. And it does seem that no one has come close to discharging this burden to date. Furthermore, if it were discharged, we would then be in a position to claim knowledge that the answers to such questions cannot be known. But assuming, as seems plausible, that such knowledge would not be based on empirical inquiries of the kind characteristic of physics or logical inquiries of the kind characteristic of mathematics, why would not its existence suffice to show the falsity of the thesis in question?

Notes

1. Of course, the relevant facts will not be independent of the existence, constitutions, etc., of believers in the special case where the beliefs or judgments in question are beliefs or judgments to the effect (e.g.) that these believers exist or are undergoing such and such mental processes. So taken strictly, the view expressed requires qualification.

2. At least provided that what the terms used in expressing the relevant proposition refer (or apply) to are not borderline cases.

3. The proof that a contradictory proposition entails the truth of every proposition is beautifully simple. It runs thus:

1. p and not-p
2. ∴ p   (from 1)
3. ∴ p v q   (from 2)
4. not-p   (from 1)
5. ∴ q   (from 3 and 4).

4. See note 2 for a necessary qualification of this claim.

5. Thus, "ideal epistemic conditions" for being justified in accepting a proposition of number theory will plausibly be quite different from "ideal epistemic conditions" for being justified in accepting a proposition of physics, or indeed certain sorts of metaphysical propositions. And, of course, what being justified in accepting a proposition under certain circumstances amounts to will be similarly relative to category of proposition, where the distinction can be made between being justified in accepting a proposition and being in ideal epistemic conditions vis-à-vis that proposition.

6. For a rich discussion of the concept of "robustness" and its relevance to confirmation theory, see W. Wimsatt, "Robustness, Reliability, and Over-determination," in Marilyn Brewer and Barry E. Collins, eds., *Scientific Inquiry and the Social Sciences* (San Francisco: Jossey-Bass, 1981).

7. See, in this connection, Jerry Fodor, *Representations* (Cambridge: MIT Press, 1981), chap. 10.

8. Not "could be false for all we know" (i.e., "we do not know they are not false")—the epistemic sense of 'could be false'—but rather "could be false" in the sense that there is nothing contradictory involved in any such set of beliefs being false.

9. By 'criteria of intelligibility' I have in mind the matters to which Einstein alludes when he speaks of the "inner perfection" of a theory. (See Paul Schilpp, ed., *Albert Einstein: Philosopher-Scientist* [Evanston: The Library of Living Philosophers, 1949], p. 223.) It involves, perhaps inter alia, "the 'naturalness' or 'logical simplicity' of the premises . . . [which in turn involves] a kind of reciprocal weighing of incommensurable quantities" (ibid.). In this connection, Einstein notes that the scientist will seem "an unscrupulous opportunist" (ibid, p. 684), since sometimes he will emphasize one virtue and sometimes a different one, no one being generally overriding. Intelligibility, he also notes, involves guidance by background principles that are "freely chosen" (ibid., p. 49). All of the passages from Einstein are quoted in Richard Miller, *Fact and Method* (Princeton: Princeton University Press, 1987), p. 445 f.

10. Ludwig Wittgenstein, *On Certainty,* trans. D. Paul and G. E. M. Anscombe (New York: Harper Torchbooks, 1969), sec. 613.

11. Ibid., sec. 614.

12. Ibid., sec. 616 (italics his).

13. Cf. Norman Malcolm, *Knowledge and Certainty* (Englewood Cliffs: Prentice-Hall, 1963), pp. 200–01.

14. A full defense of this claim is not appropriate here. Suffice it to say that

a good deal can be said by way of making this claim plausible. See, for example, Wittgenstein, *Philosophical Investigations*; and Saul Kripke, *Wittgenstein on Rules and Private Language* (Cambridge: Harvard University Press, 1982).

15. Their beliefs include (a) a belief that certain members of their community are witches in the sense of having the power to exert by "occult" means a harmful influence on others; (b) a belief that this power is rooted in an organic condition that is inherited; (c) a belief that the best way of detecting the influence of witchcraft and of identifying witches is by appealing to the revelations of oracles; and (d) a belief that one can counteract the influence of a witch or protect oneself from the harm directed at one by a witch by performing certain rites, using certain ritualistically prepared medicines, etc. See Peter Winch, "Understanding Primitive Society," *American Philosophical Quarterly* 1 (1964).

16. The line of thought in this paragraph is similar in some ways to that suggested by Donald Davidson in "On the Very Idea of a Conceptual Scheme," *Proceedings and Addresses of the American Philosophical Association* 47 (1973/74). But the kinds of limits on understanding the alien to which Wittgenstein so frequently alludes in his later writings also underlie it. See, for example, *Philosophical Investigations,* trans. G. E. M. Anscombe, 3rd ed. (New York: The Macmillan Co., 1958), secs. 206, 207 and passim. See also L. Wittgenstein, *On Certainty,* secs. 609 ff.

17. This terminology is Hilary Putnam's. See his paper "How to be an Internal Realist and a Transcendental Idealist (at the Same Time)," in R. Haller and W. Grassl, eds., *Language, Logic, and Philosophy* (Vienna: Holder-Pehler-Tempsky, 1980), pp. 101–02.

18. This terminology is also Putnam's. See ibid.

19. The notion of "reflective equilibrium" employed here is adapted from John Rawls, *A Theory of Justice* (Cambridge: Harvard University press, 1971), pp. 48–49.

20. It may be that for certain kinds of propositions, the distinction between (a) and (b) will disappear. Perhaps for mathematical propositions, for example, to be in ideal epistemic conditions vis-à-vis p (the proposition, say, that there are an infinite number of twin primes) is just to have a valid proof of p. If so, then being in such conditions *is* to have adequate justification for accepting p. Plausibly, the distinction holds, however, in the case of propositions of physics. Thus to be in ideal epistemic conditions as regards a proposition concerning the structure of space-time will just be to possess all the (conceivably obtainable) relevant observational data for determining the structure of space-time. In that case, what view about its structure was justifiable would plausibly be thought a further question.

21. Hilary Putnam makes this implication of the second case explicit in his paper "How to be an Internal Realist and a Transcendental Idealist (at the Same Time)," p. 106 f. See also his *Reason, Truth and History*, pp. 60 ff.

22. The following argument was suggested to me by the line of thought in Alvin Plantinga, "How to Be an Anti-Realist," *Proceedings and Addresses of the American Philosophical Association* 56 (1982), sec. 3.

23. Formally, the argument in the text can be expressed as follows:

1. $\Box (A \supset ((C \equiv D))$
2. $\Box (B \supset D)$
3. $\therefore \Box ((A \cdot B) \supset C)$
4. B
5. $\therefore A \supset C$
6. $-C$
7. $\therefore -A,$

where 'A' is short for:

p is true iff [if there is (or were) an ideal rational inquirer in ideal epistemic conditions, then he or she accepts (or would accept) *p*];

'B' is short for:

If there is an ideally rational inquirer in ideal epistemic conditions, then he or she accepts C;

'C' is short for:

There is an ideally rational inquirer in ideal epistemic conditions;

and 'D' is short for:

If there is (or were) an ideally rational inquirer in ideal epistemic conditions, then he or she accepts (or would accept) C.

To see the force of Premise 1, put 'C' for '*p*' in A. This yields 'C is true iff D'. But 'C is true' holds iff C. Thus, 'C iff D' is true, given A. So $\Box (A \supset (C \equiv D))$. Premises 2 and 4 are obvious, or at least plausible. Premise 3 follows from 1 and 2, and Premise 5 from 3 and 4. Premise 6 is at least plausible; at any rate it is more plausible that $-A$ than that C.

24. I borrow this phrase from Jerry Fodor, *Representations*, p. 264 and passim.

25. See Thomas Nagel, *Mortal Questions* (Cambridge: Cambridge University Press, 1979), chap. 12 ("What is it like to be a bat?").

Glossary

The intended audience for this book will have a reasonable grasp of most of the technical notions employed in it. But since a few of these may be unfamiliar to some readers and in the interest of making the book more accessible, I here give brief explanations of the terms that may prove troublesome. Some of the expressions used in the definitions are themselves defined elsewhere in this glossary; whenever this is the case, I place an asterisk before the expression(s) in question.

all-or-nothing relation   An all-or-nothing relation is a relation that cannot hold between x and y only to some degree. Thus, the relation *being the square root of* (i.e., $xy[x$ is the square root of $y]$ in Quine's notation) is all-or-nothing, whereas the relation *being loved by* (i.e., xy [x is loved by y] is not, since one can be loved by another a little or a lot.

analysandum (plural: **analysanda**)   An analysandum is an expression (or concept) that an analysis or definition provides (or purports to provide) the analysis or definition of. It is what is subjected to analysis when an analysis or definition of some term or expression is given or sought.

analysans (plural: *analysantia)*   An analysans is an expression by reference to which a term (or concept) is analyzed. Thus if the term 'vixen' is analyzed to mean the same as the expression 'female fox', the latter expression is the analysans in this analysis.

analytic truth   An analytic truth is a statement whose truth is a function solely of the meanings of the expressions it contains.

"Vixens are female foxes" would count as analytic by those who agree that there are such truths.

a priori truth   An a priori truth is a statement that can be known to be true "independently of experience," i.e., without making any observations or inferences from observation. "7 + 5 = 12" is usually taken to be a paradigm case of a truth of this kind.

asymmetric relation   A dyadic (i.e., two-place) relation R is an asymmetric relation if for all x and y in the *field of R, $xRy \supset yRx$.

biconditional   If two statements are connected by a biconditional, then either they are both true or they are both false. This statement connective is often expressed by the use of the expression *'iff'.

bivalence   The principle of bivalence holds for some statement (or class of statements) just in case it (or each member of the class) cannot fail to be determinately true or determinately false.

borderline case   A borderline case of a term (or concept) is some object or phenomenon such that the term (or concept) in question neither applies nor fails to apply to this object or phenomenon. Consider the concept expressed by the words 'was shot in New Hampshire' (C). Then a man who, while standing in New Hampshire, was shot by a man standing in Vermont would be borderline case of C.

categorical structure of the world   This expression refers to the basic scheme of most general concepts that the correct theory of the nature of reality essentially involves. Notions like *space, time, causality,* and *substance* are frequently thought to be part of the categorical structure of the world in this sense.

circular analysis   A circular analysis is one in which the concept being analyzed appears—explicitly or implicitly—in the *analysans. An analysis of the idea of causality that involves reference to laws of nature will be circular if the correct analysis of the idea of a law of nature involves reference to the concept of causality.

compossible/incompossible   Two statements (or states of affairs) are said to be compossible when they (logically) can both be true (or obtain). When they cannot, they are said to be incompossible.

concept nativism   Concept nativism is the doctrine that all (or virtually all) concepts that are expressed monomorphemically in a natural language come to be possessed by native speakers of that language as a result of some triggering mechanism, rather than by a process of learning. Such concepts, accordingly, are native to the speakers of the language in something like the way that blood type and eye color are native.

contingent truth/fact   A contingent truth (or fact) is one that (logically) could have failed to hold, i.e., its holding is not a matter of necessity. That RC is 6'2" today is a contingent truth since it could have failed to hold.

converse (of a relation)   The converse of a relation R is the relation S such that xSy if and only if yRx. *Being a parent of* is the converse of the relation *being an offspring of* since it is true that *a* is a parent of *b* if and only if *b* is an offspring of *a*.

deductive argument   A deductive argument purports to be an argument such that the conclusion follows logically from the premises, i.e., an argument such that if the premises are true, then the conclusion cannot fail to be true.

deductive inference   A deductive inference is an inference to a conclusion from a set of premises that is (or purports to be) sanctioned by the principles of deductive logic.

doxastic state   A doxastic state is a state of belief concerning some matter.

entailment   Entailment is the relation that holds between two propositions when one logically follows from the other. The proposition that follows logically is said to be entailed by the other.

epistemic sense of 'possible'   To hold that *p* is possible in the epistemic sense is to hold that *p* is not known to be false. The epistemic sense is sometimes contrasted with the metaphysical sense, according to which to hold that *p* is possible is to hold that *not-p* is not a *necessary truth.

epistemically privileged position   One is in an epistemically privileged position as regards some fact or phenomenon just in case one is in a better position to know the fact, or know about the phenomenon, in question than is anyone else.

equivalence relation   An equivalence relation is a relation that is *transitive, *symmetric, and *reflexive. And example of such a relation is the relation of being simultaneous with.

essentialism   Essentialism is the doctrine that each thing that exists has some of its properties essentially. I.e., for some of the (*purely qualitative) properties of anything that exists, it is true that there is no possible world in which that thing exists and lacks the properties in question.

field of a relation   The domain of a relation R is the set of things x for which there exists at least one y such that xRy holds. The converse domain of a relation R is the set of things y for which there exists at least one x such that xRy. The field of a relation is the logical sum of its domain and its converse domain.

haecceity   A thing has a haecceity just in case it has an *individual essence and that individual essence is not analyzable by reference either to *purely qualitative properties or to the property of having originated from such and such.

historical properties   The historical properties of an object are the properties it has in virtue of having had such and such a history. Thus having been in George Washington's pocket at a certain time or having been slept in by Grover Cleveland might be among something's historical properties.

individual essence   The individual essence of a thing consists in that property (or that set of properties) such that (a) there is no possible world in which that thing exists and lacks the property (or properties) in question, and (b) anything that exists in any possible world which has the property (or properties) in question is identical with that thing.

iff   'Iff' is a standard abbreviation for the phrase 'if and only if'.

inference to the best explanation   An inference to the best explanation is an inference to some conclusion from a set of premises on the basis of the fact that the state of affairs the conclusion records is the best explanation of the states of affairs the premises record.

irreflexive relation   A dyadic relation R is irreflexive if xRx never holds. The relation of being less than that holds between various whole numbers is irreflexive.

judgment-token and judgment-type [See *sentence-token and sentence-type*.]

Leibniz's Law   Leibniz's Law states that if something x is identical with something y, then whatever is true of x is true of y.

Leibnizian essentialism   This expression refers to the doctrine that for each thing that exists, it is true that all of its properties are essential to it.

mereological sum 'Mereology' refers to the logic of wholes and parts. The mereological sum of two entities *a* and *b* is the alleged entity that has *a* and *b* as parts and parts such that any other parts of this entity are either parts of *a*, parts of *b*, or parts of both *a* and *b*. Alternatively, the mereological sum of *a* and *b* is the least inclusive entity that includes both as parts, the entity that is made up of *a* and *b* and of nothing besides.

necessary truth/fact A necessary truth (or fact) is one that (logically) could not fail to hold. That is, its holding is not a contingent matter. That 11 is a prime number is generally thought to be a necessary truth (or fact).

non-demonstrative inference A non-demonstrative inference is an inference from some set of premises to a conclusion of a kind that is not sanctioned by the principles of deductive logic, but that purports to be nonetheless a reasonable inference in the sense that the truth of the premises provides reason for thinking the conclusion to be either true or probably true. An *inference to the best explanation is one type of non-demonstrative inference.

numerical identity *x* is said to be numerically identical to *y* just in case *x* and *y* are one and the same object.

one-one relation A relation R is one-many just in case for every *y* in the converse domain (see the definition of 'field') there is a unique *x* such that *x*R*y*. A relation R is many-one just in case for every *x* in the domain (see the definition of 'field') there is a unique *y* such that *x*R*y*. A relation is one-one just in case it is at the same time one-many and many-one. Thus a one-one relation determines a one-to-one correspondence between its domain and its converse domain.

one-many relation [See the definition of 'one-one relation'.]

open sentence An open sentence is a declarative sentence in which at least one of its singular terms has been replaced by a variable. (A different variable must be used for each different singular term replaced.)

open texture A term possesses open texture just in case it is logically possible that there should be borderline cases of its application.

'Typewriter' and 'light bulb', for example, are terms that possess open texture.

pleiotropy The phenomenon whereby a change of a single gene can effect a number of ostensibly unconnected phenotypic changes—for example, changes in the eye color, toe length, and milk yield.

propositional attitude A propositional attitude is a mental state or event the linguistic specification of which necessarily involves reference to a proposition. John's belief that it is now raining is a propositional attitude. Expecting that such and such, hoping that such and such, and desiring that such and such are all also propositional attitudes.

purely qualitative property A purely qualitative property is a property that does not involve any particulars, in the way that the property of being the owner of the book on the table, for example, involves a certain book.

qualitative identity Something x is qualitatively identical with something y just in case x and y, though distinct things, share all (or virtually all) their *purely qualitative properties.

reductive analysis A concept C has a reductive analysis just in case being an instance of C *consists* in being an instance of the analyzing condition. Thus the concept being a vixen has a reductive analysis since being a vixen just consists in being a female fox.

reflexive relation A dyadic relation R is reflexive provided xRx holds for all x within a previously fixed domain (see the definition of 'field'). Identity is a paradigm case of a reflexive relation.

relational property A relational property of something x is a property x has of being related in some way to some definite object. Thus, the property of loving John is one of Mary's relational properties.

rigid designator A rigid designator is a singular term that refers to the same object in every possible world relative to which it has a referent. Proper names, like 'John F. Kennedy', are often thought to be rigid designators. So also are expressions like '9' and 'the square root of 2'.

self-intimating state. A mental state is self-intimating just in case the being that is in that state cannot fail to be aware either that it is in the state in question or what that state's essential features are.

sentence-token/sentence-type   A sentence-token is a string of marks (or sounds) that counts as a sentence of some language, natural or artificial. Thus, the collection of ink marks between the single quotation marks following the next colon constitutes a sentence-token: 'He slept'. A judgment-token is a particular event that counts as someone's judgment that *p*. A sentence-type is the abstract entity that is instantiated by two or more tokens of the same sentence. When one says that List L below contains only one sentence, one is referring to the sentence-type each sentence on L exemplifies:

> List L: a. He slept.
> b. He slept.
> c. He slept.

A judgment-type is the abstract entity that is instantiated by two or more tokens of the same judgment.

singular proposition   A singular proposition is a proposition that essentially involves reference to one or more individuals

sub specie aeternitatis   This is a Latin phrase that is usually translated *under the aspect of eternity*. To look at some phenomenon *sub specie aeternitatis* is to see it, as it were, from God's point of view and not from a perspective defined by some particular position in space or time or conditioned by facts that could have been otherwise.

symmetric relation   A dyadic relation R is symmetric just in case it is true for all *x* and *y* in the *field of R that $xRy \supset yRx$. *Being similar to* is a symmetric relation.

time-indexed property   P is a time-indexed property just in case the linguistic expression of P essentially involves a singular term that designates a moment or stretch of time. Being-fat-at-t (or $x[x$ is fat at t]) is a time-indexed property.

transcendental idealism   This expression refers to the Kantian view that the basic features of the world of nature that we ordinarily believe to exist independently of us—in particular its spatial and temporal characteristics and the fact that it exhibits causal structure—depend upon (and reflect) the structure of our minds.

transitive relation   A dyadic relation R is transitive provided it is true that whenever *xRy* and *yRz* hold, *xRz* also holds. The relation of being less than (among whole numbers) is transitive.

truth-conditions   The truth-conditions of a declarative sentence (or a statement or proposition) consist of the conditions (or states of affairs) that are (logically) both severally necessary and jointly sufficient for its being the case that the sentence (statement, proposition) is true. They are, in other words, the conditions that make the sentence (statement, proposition) true, when it is true, the conditions in virtue of which it is true and in the absence of which it fails to be true (and this as a matter of logic or necessity).

truth value   The truth value of a sentence (statement, proposition) is its truth or falsity.

universal grammar   'Universal grammar' refers to an (alleged) system of grammatical rules to which all natural languages conform, despite their differences. Universal grammar is held, by its exponents, to be an innate feature of the human brain.

vagueness   A vague term is one relative to which there exist *border-line cases. The word 'bald' is vague because many heads exist which it is neither clearly correct nor clearly incorrect to describe as bald.

Suggestions for Further Reading

Chapter One: The Persistence of Persons

Chisholm, Roderick. *Person and Object*. LaSalle, Illinois: Open Court Publishing Co., 1976.

Parfit, Derek. *Reasons and Persons*. Oxford: Clarendon Press, 1984.

Perry, John, ed. *Personal Identity*. Berkeley: University of California Press, 1975.

Rorty, Amelie, ed. *The Identities of Persons*. Berkeley: University of California Press, 1976.

Shoemaker, Sydney, and Richard Swinburne. *Personal Identity*. Oxford: Basil Blackwell, 1984.

Chapter Two: Freedom, Necessity, and Chance

Albritton, Rogers. "Freedom of the Will and Freedom of Action." *Proceedings and Addresses of the American Philosophical Association* 59 (1985).

Dennett, Daniel. *Elbow Room*. Cambridge: MIT Press, 1984.

Nozick, Robert. *Philosophical Explanations*. Cambridge: Harvard University Press, 1981.

van Inwagen, Peter. *An Essay on Free Will*. Oxford: Clarendon Press, 1983.

Watson, Gary, ed. *Free Will*. Oxford: Oxford University Press, 1982.

Chapter Three: Materialism and the Mental

Block, Ned, ed. *Readings in the Philosophy of Psychology*, 2 volumes. Cambridge: Harvard University Press, 1980, 1981.

Churchland, Paul. *Matter and Consciousness*. Cambridge: MIT Press, 1984.

Dennett, Daniel. *Brainstorms*. Montgomery, Vermont: Bradford, 1978.

Nagel, Thomas. *The View from Nowhere*. New York: Oxford University Press, 1986.

Popper, Karl and John Eccles. *The Self and Its Brain*. New York: Springer-Verlag, 1977.

Chapter Four: The Possible and the Actual

Forrest, Peter, and D. M. Armstrong. "An Argument Against David Lewis' Theory of Possible Worlds." *Australasian Journal of Philosophy* 62 (1984).

Lewis, David. *Philosophical Papers*. Vol. 1. (New York: Oxford University Press, 1983).

———. *On the Plurality of Worlds*. Oxford: Basil Blackwell, 1986.

Loux, Michael, ed. *The Possible and the Actual*. Ithaca: Cornell University Press, 1979.

McGinn, Colin. "Modal Reality." In Richard Healey, ed., *Reduction, Time and Reality*. Cambridge: Cambridge University Press, 1981.

Chapter Five: Essences, Origins, and Branching Worlds

Forbes, Graeme. *The Metaphysics of Modality*. Oxford: Clarendon Press, 1985.

French, Peter A., Theodore Uehling, Jr., and Howard K. Wettstein, eds. *Midwest Studies in Philosophy*, Vol. 11: *Studies in Essentialism*. Minneapolis: University of Minnesota Press, 1986.

Kripke, Saul. *Naming and Necessity*. Cambridge: Harvard University Press, 1980.

Plantinga, Alvin. *The Nature of Necessity*. Oxford: Clarendon Press, 1974.

Salmon, Nathan. *Reference and Essence*. Princeton: Princeton University Press, 1981.

Chapter Six: The Passage of Time

Gale, Richard, ed. *The Philosophy of Time*. Garden City, N.Y.: Anchor Books, 1967.

Grünbaum, Adolf. *Philosophical Problems of Space and Time.* 2nd ed. Dordrecht: D. Reidel, 1973.

Mellor, D. H. *Real Time.* Cambridge: Cambridge University Press, 1981.

Schlesinger, George. *Aspects of Time.* Indianapolis: Hackett Publishing Co., 1980.

Smart, J. J. C., ed. *Problems of Space and Time.* New York: The Macmillan Co., 1964.

Chapter Seven: Metaphysical Theology and the Life of Faith

O'Hear, Anthony. *Experience, Explanation and Faith.* London: Routledge & Kegan Paul, 1984.

Phillips, D. Z. *The Concept of Prayer.* New York: Schocken Books, 1966.

Plantinga, Alvin, and Nicholas Wolterstorff, eds. *Faith and Rationality: Reason and Belief in God.* Notre Dame: University of Notre Dame Press, 1983.

Swinburne, Richard. *The Existence of God.* Oxford: Clarendon Press, 1979.

Wittgenstein, Ludwig. *Culture and Value,* trans. P. Winch. Chicago: University of Chicago Press, 1980.

Chapter Eight: Truth, Epistemological Optimism, and the Limits of Science

Alston, William. "Yes, Virginia, There Is a Real World." *Proceedings and Addresses of the American Philosophical Association* 52 (1979).

Dummett, Michael. *Truth and Other Enigmas.* Cambridge: Harvard University Press, 1978.

Putnam, Hilary. *Reason, Truth and History.* Cambridge: Cambridge University Press, 1981.

Rorty, Richard. *Consequences of Pragmatism.* Minneapolis: University of Minnesota Press, 1982.

Wittgenstein, Ludwig. *On Certainty,* trans. D. Paul and G. E. M. Anscombe. New York: Harper & Row, 1969.

Index